The Glossary of Key Purchasing Terms, Acronyms, and Formulas

Compiled by:
Janet L. Przirembel

PT Publications, Inc.
Suite 100
3109 45th Street
West Palm Beach, FL 33407

Library of Congress Cataloging-in-Publication Data

The glossary of key purchasing terms, acronyms, and formulas /
P.T. Publications, Inc. ; [Editor, Janet L. Przirembel].
        p. cm.
Includes bibliographical references.
ISBN 0-945456-22-0 (pbk.)
    1.Purchasing -- Terminology. I. Przirembel, Janet L. II. PT
Publications, Inc.
HF5437.G57   1995
658.7'2'03--dc20   95-39697
                                                            CIP

Table of Contents

This edition of **The Glossary of Key Purchasing Terms, Acronyms, and Formulas** was prepared by PT Publications.

Editorial

Kevin Grieco, Vice President

Janet L. Przirembel, Editor

Leslie Boyce, Administration

The information in this book was obtained from the following sources:
(See Bibliography for complete publication information.)

Glossary of Key Purchasing Terms

Just-In-Time Purchasing: In Pursuit of Excellence

Oracle Purchasing™ Reference Manual Release 10, Volume 4

Performance Measurements: A Roadmap for Excellence

Supplier Certification II: A Handbook for Achieving Excellence Through Continuous Improvement

Supply Management Toolbox: How to Manage Your Suppliers

Professionals for Technology Associates, Inc. Statistical Process Control Seminar

The World of Negotiations: Never Being a Loser

Mr. John Choate

Preface

The purchasing field is filled with a multitude of buzz words and equations ... Supplier Certification (SC), Just-In-Time (J.I.T.), Total Quality Control (TQC), Suppliers as Partners (SAP), $UCL_{\bar{x}} = X + A_2\bar{R}$. What do these terms and formulas mean? These definitions, as well as other acronyms and purchasing performance formulas, can be found in this book.

This glossary is designed to be a comprehensive reference guide for purchasing professionals at all levels. In a simple, logical fashion, it presents concise and germane definitions of purchasing terminology.

The definitions and information contained in this book were collected from the many sources listed on the back page of this dictionary.

It was reviewed by several experts in the field of purchasing from many companies and organizations worldwide. Their suggestions, additions and improvements were incorporated into the original list of terms collected by the editor.

With special appreciation for their cooperation, Carl Cooper, Senior Applications Consultant, Motorola; Charles Perry, General Manager, ITT; Pierre Gosselin, Senior Vice President – Purchasing and Procurement, ABB; Denise Gillespie, Director of Materials, Xomed; John Semanik with the NAPM San Jose Chapter; and Peter L. Grieco, Jr., CEO, Professionals for Technology Associates, Inc.

With special thanks to Larry Ellison, CEO, and Ron Wohl, Senior Vice President, at the Oracle Corporation, for permission to include the terms from the *Oracle Purchasing*™ *Reference Manual;* to Executive Vice President R. Jerry Baker and Senior Vice President Paul Novack at the National Association of Purchasing Management (NAPM) for permission to incorporate the terms from NAPM's *Glossary of Key Purchasing Terms* to provide you with a world class glossary, and to John Choate who supplied many of the terms listed in the glossary.

A

A_2 – A multiplier of $\overline{R}$ used to calculate the control limits for averages.

ABC CLASSIFICATION – Stratification of inventory items in decreasing order of annual dollar volume. This array is then split into three classes, called A, B, and C. Class A contains the items with the highest annual dollar volume and receives the most attention. The medium Class B receives less attention, and Class C, which contains the low dollar volume items, is controlled routinely.

ABSTRACT OF TITLE – A condensed history of the title to property, based on past records.

ACCEPT – An action that you take to indicate that you accept the previous approver's authorization.

ACCEPTANCE SAMPLING – A statistical quality control technique used to evaluate the overall condition of a given lot by inspecting only a portion or sample of the lot.

ACCOUNTING PERIOD – The fiscal period a company uses to report financial results, such as a calendar month or fiscal period.

ACCOUNTS PAYABLE ACCRUAL ACCOUNT – The account used to accrue your payable liabilities when you receive your items. Always used for inventory and outside processing purchases. You can also accrue expenses at the time of receipt. Used by Purchasing and Inventory, the accounts payable account represents your uninvoiced receipts and is included in your month end accounts payable liability balance. This account balance is cleared when the invoice is matched in Payables.

ACCRUAL ACCOUNTING – Recognition of revenue when you sell goods and recognition of expenses when a supplier provides services or goods. Accrual based accounting matches expenses with associated revenues when you receive the benefit of the goods and services rather than when cash is paid or received.

ACCRUED RECEIPTS ACCOUNT – The account used to accrue your uninvoiced expense receipts at month end by Purchasing. The accrued receipts account may or may not be the same account as the accounts payable accrual account. However, both accrual accounts represent additional payable liabilities that you include in your month end accounts payable liability balance. You reverse the accrued receipts account by reversing the month end journal in the following period.

ACKNOWLEDGMENT – A communication by a supplier to advise a purchaser that a purchase order has been received. It usually implies acceptance of the order by the supplier.

ACQUISITION COST – In the context of Economic Order Quantity (E.O.Q.) analysis, the acquisition cost includes all costs associated with generating and processing an order and its related paperwork.

In a broader management sense, the acquisition cost is the sum of the ordering, transporting, handling, and all inventory holding costs associated with the acquisition of material.

ACTION MESSAGE – An output of an Material Requirements Planning (MRP I) system that identifies the need for and the type of action to be taken to correct a current or potential material coverage problem.

ACTIVE INVENTORY – Covers raw material, work-in-process, and finished products which will be used or sold within the budgeted period without extra cost or loss.

ACTIVITY BASED COSTING (ABC) – A system for searching out cost drivers and assigning them directly to products and services. Frequently used to drive improvement efforts by monitoring and controlling activities in order to bring true costs into the open.

ACTUAL COSTS – Those labor and material costs which are charged to a job as it moves through the production process.

AD VALOREM (ACCORDING TO VALUE) – A term usually applied to a customs duty charged on the *value only* of goods that are dutiable, irrespective of quality, weight, or any other considerations. The ad valorem rates of duty are expressed in percentage of the value of the goods, usually ascertained from the invoice.

ADMINISTERED PRICE – A price determined by the conscious price policy of a seller rather than by the competitive forces of the market place.

ADVANCE ARRANGEMENT – An advance agreement required for the movement of certain commodities by air carrier. Gold and other precious metals, live animals, and other classes of shipments may require such arrangements.

ADVANCE BUYING – Advance buying (also called forward buying) is the commitment of purchases in anticipation of future requirements beyond current lead times. Organizations may buy ahead as a matter of strategy or because of anticipated shortages, strikes, or price increases.

ADVANCED CHARGE – The amount of freight or other charge on a shipment advanced by one transportation line to another, or to the shipper, to be collected from the consignee.

AFFIDAVIT – A written statement sworn to and acknowledged by a notary.

AFFIRMATIVE ACTION – A provision of the Equal Opportunity Act of 1972 that requires all firms to take "affirmative action" to move toward achieving a work force that accurately reflects the composition of the community. A firm must compare its employment, by department and by job level, with data on the availability of talent in the relevant labor market.

AGENCY – This term defines the legal relationship that exists between two parties by which one is authorized to perform or transact specified business activities for the other.

AGENT – Legally, an agent is a person or organization authorized to act for another person or organization in prescribed dealings with a third party.

AGGREGATE FORECAST – An estimate of sales for some grouping of products; perhaps for all products produced by some manufacturing facility.

AGGREGATE INVENTORY – The sum of the inventory levels for individual items. For example, the aggregate finished goods inventory would be made up of one-half the sum of all the lot sizes plus the sum of all of the safety stocks plus anticipated inventory plus transportation inventory.

AIR WAY BILL – The document used for the shipment of air freight by national and international air carriers that states the commodities shipped, shipping instruction, shipping costs, etc.

ALPHANUMERIC NUMBER TYPE – An option for numbering documents, employees, and suppliers where assigned numbers can contain letters as well as numbers.

ALTERNATE ROUTING – A routing, usually less preferred than the normal routing, but delivering identical end-products.

AMOUNT BASED ORDER – An order you place, receive, and pay based solely on the amount of the service that you purchase.

ANNUALIZED CONTRACTS – A method of acquiring materials that helps ensure continuous supply of material, minimizes forward commitments, and provides the supplier with estimated future requirements.

ANSI X12 – A set of standards promulgated by the American National Standards Institute for use in formatting and handling purchasing related documents transmitted by electronic data interchange (EDI).

ANTICIPATION INVENTORY – Anticipation stocks are accumulated for a well defined future need. They differ from buffer (safety) stock in that they are committed in the face of certainty.

APPRAISAL COSTS – Costs associated with ensuring that products conform to requirements. Activities in this area are typical of traditional quality methods and include testing, inspection and material review boards.

APPROVAL LIST – A formal list of those suppliers that have been evaluated and deemed capable of satisfactory performance.

APPROVE – An action that you take to indicate that you consider the contents of the purchasing document to be correct. If the document passes the submission tests and if you have sufficient authority, Purchasing approves the document.

APPROVED – A purchase order or requisition status that indicates a user with the appropriate authorization approved the purchase or requisition. Purchasing verifies that the purchase order or requisition is complete during the approval process.

ARBITRAGE – A financial term meaning the simultaneous buying of a security, commodity, or currency in one market while selling the same item in another. The key to arbitrage is taking advantage of temporary aberrations in the market.

ARBITRATION – A means of settling disputes between parties with an objective outside party acting as a fact finder and primary decision maker.

ARCHIVING – The process of recording all historical versions of approved purchase orders. Purchasing automatically archives a purchase order when you approve it for the first time. Purchasing subsequently archives your purchase orders during the approval process if you have increased the revision number since the last time you approved the purchase order.

ARRIVAL DATE – The date purchased material is due to arrive at the receiving site. Arrival date can be input, can be equal to the current due date, or can be calculated from ship date plus transit time. (Syn. expected receipt date)

ASSEMBLY – A group of subassemblies and/or parts that are put together. The total unit constitutes a major consolidation of the final product. An assembly may be an end item or a component of a higher level assembly. (See: component, subassembly)

ASSIGNMENT – A transference of a property right (such as a contract or a purchase order) or title to another party. In shipping, it is commonly used with a bill of lading which involves transfer of rights, title and interest for the purpose of endorsement. Such endorsement gives, to the party named, the title to the property covered by the bill of lading.

ATTACHMENT – A legal proceeding accompanying an action in court by which a plaintiff may acquire a lien on a defendant's property as a security for the payment of any judgement which the plaintiff may obtain.

AUDIT – A process to determine whether a supplier's quality and manufacturing processes are under control. Audits are also used as a method to improve a supplier's performance by pointing out weaknesses.

AUTHORIZATION CHECK – A set of tests on a purchasing document to determine if the document approver has sufficient authority to perform the approval action.

AUTOMATIC NUMBERING – A numbering option to let Purchasing assign numbers to your documents, employees, or suppliers automatically.

AUTOSOURCING – A Purchasing feature that allows you to specify for predefined items a list of approved suppliers and to associate source documents for these suppliers. When you create a requisition or purchase order line for the item, Purchasing automatically provides appropriate pricing for the specified quantity based on the top-ranked open source document for the top-ranked supplier.

AVAILABLE MATERIAL – A term usually interpreted to mean "material available for planning," and thus including not only the on hand inventory, but also inventory on order. Material "available to promise" would, of course, be only the material on hand that has not been assigned.

AVAILABLE WORK – Work that is actually in a department ready to be worked on, as opposed to scheduled work that may not yet be on hand.

B

BACKDOOR SELLING – Bypassing of the purchasing department by a sales person who goes directly to the department or end user of the product being purchased.

BACKLOG – All of the customer orders booked, i.e., received but not yet shipped. Sometimes referred to as "open orders."

BACK ORDER – An unfilled customer order or commitment. It is an immediate (or past due) demand against an item whose inventory is insufficient to satisfy the demand.

BACKWARD SCHEDULING – A scheduling technique where the schedule is computed starting with the due date for the order and working backward to determine the required start date. This can generate negative times, thereby identifying where time must be made up. (Ant. forward scheduling)

BALANCED LOADING – Loading a starting department with a product mix that should not overload or underload subsequent departments.

BANK(ER'S) ACCEPTANCE – An instrument used in financing foreign trade, making possible the payment of cash to an exporter covering all or part of the amount of a shipment made by him.

BAR CODE – A pattern of alternating parallel bars and spaces, representing numbers and other characters that are machine readable. The major advantages of using bar coding technology in receiving and stores operations are the reductions in error rate and improved entry speed and count accuracy.

BARTER – The act of exchanging one good or service for another, as distinct from trading by use of currency. Barter is a form of countertrade sometimes used in international business.

"BASED-ON" PRICE – A price derived from adequate price competition, resulting directly from a competitive solicitation or from price analysis, that demonstrates the "based-on" price is fair and reasonable when compared with current or recent prices paid for the same or substantially the same items.

BASE-STOCK SYSTEM – In its simplest form, a base-stock system is an inventory system in which a replenishment order is issued each time a withdrawal is made and the order quantity is equal to the amount of the withdrawal. This type of system is commonly referred to as a par-stock system (bringing stock back to par level).

BASE UNIT – The unit of measure to which you convert all units of measure within one class. The base unit is the smallest or most commonly used unit of measure in the class. For example, millimeter is the base unit in the Length class. You define your base unit of measure when you create your unit class.

BASIC ORDERING AGREEMENT (B.O.A.) – An unfunded instrument that permits repetitive purchases to be made on an order-by-order basis from suppliers, usually awarded on a competitive basis for a prescribed period of time. The holders are required by specifications, terms, and conditions to provide specified goods and/or services at predetermined prices.

BENCHMARK – A standard or point of reference used in measuring or judging quality, value, performance, price, etc. Benchmarks of purchasing performance, such as "purchasing operating expenses as a percent of company sales dollars," give purchasing professionals a reference point that can be used to evaluate their own firm's performance.

BENCHMARKING – A strategic and managerial tool for identifying and emulating those companies who excel in a particular business area. Benchmarking is a continuous process whereby a company adopts the best-in-class practices of World Class companies.

"BEST BUY" – A term used to imply that a purchase represents an overall combination of quality, price, and various elements of required service that in total are optimal relative to the firm's needs.

BID – A price, whether for payment or acceptance. A quotation specifically given to a prospective purchaser upon their request, usually in competition with other suppliers.

BID ANALYSIS – Analysis of the provisions of a bid, usually for the purpose of comparing the strengths and weaknesses of the various bids received.

BID BOND – See Bond.

BILL OF LADING (UNIFORM) – A carrier's contract and receipt for goods which it agrees to transport from one place to another and to deliver to a designated person or assigns for compensation and upon such conditions as are stated therein.

BILL OF LABOR – A statement of the key resources required to manufacture one unit of a selected item.

Often used to predict the impact of the item scheduled in the master production schedule (MPS) on these resources. (Syn. bill of resources, resource profile)

BILL OF MATERIAL – A listing of all materials that go into a parent assembly showing the quantity of each required to make an assembly. There are a variety of formats for bills of material, including single level bill of material, indented bill of material, modular (planning), costed bill of material, etc.

BILL OF SALE – A written document formally transferring ownership of personal property specified in the document from the supplier to the purchaser.

BLANK-CHECK PURCHASE ORDER – An ordering technique that includes a bank draft as the bottom portion of the purchase order form. When the order is shipped, the supplier enters the amount due for payment on the draft and sends it to the firm's bank for deposit. Many firms that utilize this approach for numerous small purchases refer to it as a purchase order draft system.

BLANKET ORDER – A long-term commitment to a supplier for material against which short-term releases will be generated to satisfy requirements.

BLANKET RELEASE – An actual order of goods and services against a blanket purchase agreement. The blanket purchase agreement determines the characteristics and the prices of the items. The blanket release specifies the actual quantities and dates ordered for the items. You identify a blanket release by the combination of the blanket purchase agreement number and the release number.

BLIND RECEIVING – A site option that requires your receiving staff to count all items on a receipt line. Blind receiving prevents display of expected receipt quantities in Purchasing receiving forms.

BOND – A written instrument executed by a bidder or contractor (the principal) and a second party (the surety) to assure fulfillment of the principal's obligation to a third party. Although there are several types of bonds, a performance bond (completion bond), bid bond (bid guarantee) and payment bond are the most common.

A performance bond normally is accompanied by a payment bond (particularly on a construction contract) and is submitted after previous submission of a bid bond. The performance bond secures the performance and fulfillment of all undertakings, covenants, terms, conditions, and agreements contained in the contract. A bid bond assures that the bidder will not fail to execute a contract *on the basis of its bid.*

BONDED WAREHOUSE – A type of warehouse that must be approved by the U.S. Treasury Department where goods must be held until duties are paid or goods are otherwise properly released. Such warehouses are used for storage and custody of import merchandise subject to duty, or for goods to be reshipped without entry.

BOOK INVENTORY – An accounting definition of inventory units or value obtained from perpetual inventory records rather than by actual count.

BOTTLENECK – A facility, function, department, etc., that impedes production. For example, a machine or work center where jobs arrive at a faster rate than they leave.

BREACH OF WARRANTY – This occurs when the material or product fails to meet the quality or other specification warranted by the supplier.

BREAK BULK – The splitting up of one consolidated or large-volume shipment into smaller ones for ultimate delivery to consignees.

This term also is commonly used to describe the process of splitting up case quantities and selling by the each.

BREAK EVEN POINT – Point at which cost of goods sold equals sales.

BROKER – An intermediary who, for a fee, brings a buyer and seller together. Normally, a broker provides some additional service to the purchaser. The broker has no ownership of the goods being sold, with the payment and credit transactions remaining the responsibility of the seller.

BUFFER INVENTORY – See Safety Stock.

BUDGET – The financial expression of objectives. The budget includes total cash flow income and outflow.

BUSINESS AFFIRMATIVE ACTION – The process of taking special or unusual steps to assure that businesses owned by minorities and/or women will have equal access to the company's purchasing process and will obtain their fair share of awards.

BUSINESS UNIT – See Strategic Business Unit.

BUYBACK – A type of countertrade that occurs when a firm builds a plant in a foreign country (or supplies technology, equipment, training or other services) and agrees to take a certain portion of the plant's output as partial payment for investment.

BUYER – An individual who acts as an agent on behalf of his/her company in dealings with suppliers.

BUYER CODE – A code used to identify the purchasing person responsible for a given item and/or purchase order.

BUYER'S MARKET – A "buyer's market" is considered to exist when goods are readily available and when the economic forces of business tend to cause goods to be priced at the purchaser's estimate of value.

BUYER/PLANNER – A functional title given to an individual whose duties combine the production planning and procurement function into a single position, called the buyer/planner, who is in charge of a specific line of inventory. The concept is based on the idea that the same person should have the authority and responsibility for both the production planning and the purchasing decisions for specified items.

BUYING TEAM – The practice of utilizing buying teams for strategic sourcing is a method in which individuals from several departments (such as purchasing, operations, engineering, finance, etc.) pool their expertise to jointly make sourcing investigations and decisions.

C

c – The number of imperfections.

c̄ – The average number of imperfections.

CANCEL – You can cancel a purchase order after approving it. When you cancel a purchase order, you prevent anyone from adding new lines to the purchase order or receiving additional goods. Purchasing still allows billing for goods you received before cancelling the purchase order. Purchasing releases any unfilled requisition lines for reassignment to another purchase order.

CANCELLATION CHARGES – A fee charged by a seller to cover the costs associated with a customer's cancellation of an order. If the seller has started any engineering work, purchased raw materials, or started any manufacturing operations, these charges would be included in the cancellation charge.

CAPACITY – The highest sustainable output rate which can be achieved with the current product specifications, product mix, work force, plant and equipment.

CAPACITY CONTROL – The process of measuring production output and comparing it with the capacity requirements plan, determining if the variance exceeds preestablished limits, and taking corrective action to get back on plan if the limits are exceeded. (Ant. input/ output control)

CAPACITY REQUIREMENTS PLANNING (CRP) – The function of establishing, measuring, and adjusting limits or levels of capacity that are consistent with a production plan. The term capacity requirements planning in this context is the process of determining how much labor and/or machine resources are required to accomplish the tasks of production. Open shop orders, and planned orders in the Material Requirements Planning (MRP I) system, are input to CRP which "translates" these orders into hours of work by work center by time period.

CAPITAL – The resources, particularly money, available for investing in assets, particularly those of a fixed nature.

CARLOAD (C/L) – The weight and/or volume necessary to qualify for a rail carload rate, or a rail car loaded to its capacity. The carload quantity referred to on a carload rate has nothing to do with the actual quantity required to fill the rail car, but is the minimum weight specified to qualify for a lower class rate.

CARRYING COST – The costs associated with having an inventory, such as taxes, insurance, obsolescence, spoilage, and space occupied.

CARTAGE – A charge made for the hauling and transferring of goods, usually on a local basis and short haul in nature; drayage.

The word also is used to mean the physical movement of the goods.

CASH DISCOUNT – A form of discount whose purpose is to secure prompt payment of an account. The net price of the purchased item is set at a point which will yield a fair profit to the supplier and is the price the supplier expects most customers to pay. Those who do not pay within the specified time limit are expected to pay *gross* price.

CASH ON DELIVERY (C.O.D.) – Payment for purchases on delivery.

CATEGORY – Code used to group items with similar characteristics, such as plastic, metal, or glass items.

CAVEAT EMPTOR – "Let the buyer beware." The purchase is at the buyer's risk.

CAVEAT VENDITOR – "Let the seller beware." The supplier, in some situations, is liable to the buyer if the goods or services delivered are not of the same type, or the right quality, or for the purpose as described in the contract of sale.

CENTRALIZED PURCHASING – In centralized purchasing, a separate individual or department is established within the organization and given authority to make the majority of purchases.

There are numerous advantages for this type of organization of the purchasing function, including the ease of standardization of products, reduction of administrative duplication, more leverage capability due to a larger quantity of purchases, limited interdepartmental competition in times of short supply, more control over purchasing commitments, greater administrative efficiency for supplier, and the development of specialization and expertise in purchasing activities.

Centralization can be implemented in a multiple-site organization, as well as a single-site organization.

CERTIFICATE OF COMPLIANCE – A document, usually required by customs officials, identifying the country of origin of imported goods.

CHANGE ORDER – A formal notification that a purchase order or shop order has changed.

CHECK FUNDS – To certify whether you have funds available to complete your requisition or purchase order. The difference between the amount you are authorized to spend and the amount of your expenditures plus encumbrances equals your funds available. You can certify funds available at any time when you enter a requisition or a purchase order. You can track funds availability at different authority levels on-line.

CHECK WITH ORDER – See Blank-Check Purchase Order.

CISG – United Nations Convention on Contracts for the International Sale of Goods. (Also referred to as the Vienna Convention.) Effective January 1988, the terms of this convention replaced the terms of the UCC in international transactions between U.S. parties and those in other countries that have ratified the convention. CISG applies to any contract for the sale of goods made between two firms whose places of business are in different countries *which have adopted CISG.* CISG does not apply to any domestic contract for the sale of goods. As of May 1992, thirty-four countries had adopted the CISG, including the U.S.

CLASS FREIGHT RATE – A rate resulting from a classification rating of the freight. While commodity rates are available only on selected commodities, a class rate can be found for almost all commodities. Class rates were created to simplify the process of providing a specific rate for each commodity being transported.

CLOSE – To automatically close a purchase order once you receive (if you require receipt) and are billed for all purchase order shipments. Since you do not require or expect any further activity, Purchasing closes the purchase order. You can also manually close the purchase order early if you do not expect any further activity. Adding lines to a purchase order or receiving against it reopens the purchase order. Purchasing does not consider closed purchase orders for accruals.

COLLUSIVE BIDDING – An unethical and illegal practice of suppliers acting in collusion to "fix" their bids in a collectively advantageous manner. Legal action is possible, but seldom feasible due to the expense, delay and risks of the outcome.

COMMERCIAL BRIBE – A "bribe" is a gift given in advance of a transaction or service for the purpose of influencing the behavior of the other party. A purchaser's acceptance of bribes from suppliers is unethical and illegal behavior.

COMMITTED AMOUNT – The amount you agree to spend with a supplier.

COMMODITY BUYING – Grouping like parts or materials under one grouping. It may be used to control buyer's items.

COMMODITY FREIGHT RATE – A transportation rate for a specific commodity, moving between specified points, sometimes in a certain direction, and typically for a specific minimum quantity. The purpose of the commodity rate is to provide a lower rate to reflect the economic benefits to the carrier resulting from more predictable and larger scale movements over certain routes.

COMMON CARRIER – A common carrier serves all customers, but carries only the types of freight for which it is certified. The most accepted characteristics of a common transportation carrier are the availability of service to anyone seeking a transportation movement, without discrimination; the publication of rates; the provision of service on a schedule; service to designated points or within a designated area; and service for a given class(es) of movement and commodities. All common carriers are regulated to some extent by federal agencies.

COMPETITIVE BIDDING – The offer of estimates by firms or individuals competing for a contract, privilege, or right to supply specified services or merchandise.

COMPETITIVE PROPOSALS – A competitive procurement practice in government purchasing that: (1) is initiated by a request for proposals and sets out the government's requirements and criteria for proposal evaluation; (2) contemplates the submission of timely proposals by the maximum number of possible suppliers; (3) usually provides discussion with those suppliers found to be within the competitive range; and (4) concludes with the award of a contract to the one supplier whose proposal is most advantageous to the government, considering price and the other factors included in the solicitation.

COMPONENT – An inclusive term used to identify a raw material, ingredient, part, or subassembly that goes into a higher level assembly, compound, or other item.

CONCURRENT ENGINEERING – An environment in which all functional disciplines contribute to the design, development, production, distribution and sale of a product or service. The company performs these activities concurrently and cooperatively instead of sequentially.

CONCURRENT PROCESS – A task that is in the process of completing. Each time you submit a task, you create a new concurrent process. A concurrent process runs simultaneously with other concurrent processes (and other activities on your computer) to help you complete multiple tasks at once, with no interruptions to your terminal.

CONFIDENTIALITY AGREEMENT – An agreement between a company and a supplier which establishes the rights and obligations of both parties with respect to proprietary interests and data.

CONFIRMING ORDER – A purchase order issued to a supplier, listing the goods or services and terms of an order, placed verbally or otherwise, in advance of the issuance of the formal purchase document.

CONFLICT OF INTEREST – A situation in which an individual has a personal interest (or responsibility) as well as a job responsibility – and a clear possibility exists that there may be a conflict between the two. The individual's actions may be influenced by his/her personal interest to the detriment of performing the professional responsibility effectively (e.g., buying from a supplier owned by a family member).

CONSIGNED STOCKS – Inventories which are in the possession of customers, dealers, agents, etc., but remain the property of the manufacturer by agreement.

CONSIGNEE – The person or organization to whom a shipper directs the carrier to deliver goods, generally the purchaser of the goods.

CONSIGNMENT BUYING – A method of procurement in which a supplier maintains an inventory on the premises of the purchaser. The purchaser's obligation to pay for the goods begins when goods are drawn from the stock for use.

CONSIGNOR – The shipper of a transportation movement.

CONSOLIDATION – Combining less-than-truckload or less-than-carload shipments from various facilities at a centrally located point, and transporting them as a larger shipment, typically at a lower freight rate.

CONTAINERIZATION – The practice of utilizing large, sealed, standard-size containers primarily for intermodal and international shipping. The containers can be transloaded between rail, motor, and water carriers to reduce transit time, theft, packaging requirements, damage and usually costs.

CONTINUOUS IMPROVEMENT PROCESS – A process whereby a company uses problem-solving techniques to eliminate waste.

CONTINUOUS REVIEW SYSTEM – A popular inventory control system in which the remaining quantity of an item is reviewed either manually or by computer each time a withdraw is made from inventory to determine whether it is time to reorder.

CONTRACT – An agreement between two or more competent persons to perform a specific act or acts. A contract may be verbal or written. A purchase order, when accepted by a supplier, becomes a contract. Acceptance may be in writing or by performance.

CONTRACT ADMINISTRATION – Those activities and actions taken by the buyer and supplier during the time from contract award to contract closeout. They may include follow-up, expediting, and many supplier management functions.

CONTRACT CARRIER – A contract carrier, regardless of mode, provides transportation and/or related services according to a contractual agreement. Tariff rates do not apply to contract transportation service, and contract rates will generally be lower than regular common carrier rates.

CONTRACT DATE – The date when a contract is accepted by all parties.

CONTRACT TYPE – Normally refers to the pricing terms of the agreement between buyer and seller. Thus a contract may be a "fixed-price" type or a "cost-reimbursement" type.

CONVERSION FORMULA – The number that, when multiplied by the quantity of one unit of the source base unit, gives you the quantity of one unit of the destination base units in the interclass conversion. The number is also the conversion between units for standard unit conversion or item-specific conversion.

COOPERATIVE PURCHASING – A purchasing approach used primarily by institutions in which a group of institutions form or utilize centralized buying service that purchases specified types of items for all institutional members of the group. The resulting volume buying usually produces significant cost savings for group members. Educational and Institutional Cooperative Service, Inc. (E&I) is perhaps the largest and most well known cooperative purchasing organization.

CORRELATION – The relationship between two sets of numbers, such as between two quantities, such that when one changes, the other is likely to make a corresponding change. If the changes are in the same direction, there is a positive correlation. When changes tend to go in opposite directions, there is a negative correlation.

COST– The total amount of money spent to produce a product or service at a specific time and place.

COST ANALYSIS – A review and an evaluation of actual or anticipated cost data (material, labor, overhead, G&A). This analysis involves applying experience, knowledge, and judgment to date in an attempt to project reasonable estimated contract costs. Estimated costs serve as the basis for buyer-seller negotiation which will arrive at mutually agreeable contract prices.

COST AND FREIGHT (C&F) – Under this arrangement, when a supplier quotes a price for the goods being sold, it includes the cost of the transportation to the named point of destination; it is used most commonly in international shipping.

COST AVOIDANCE– A purchasing action by means of which certain material/supplier increases are not incurred by the purchasing firm. Since it is not always possible to reduce existing costs, cost "avoidances" often are reported as savings when measuring or evaluating purchasing performance.

COST CENTER – The smallest segment of an organization for which costs are collected, such as the lathe department. The criteria in defining cost centers are that the cost be significant and the area of responsibility be clearly defined.

COST FACTORS – The units of input that represent costs to the manufacturing system. For example: labor hours, purchased material.

COST, INSURANCE, AND FREIGHT (C.I.F.) – A sales practice in international trade whereby the supplier quotes a price that includes the cost of the material, freight charges to a destination point, and marine insurance en route.

COST-PLUS – A pricing method whereby the purchaser agrees to pay the supplier an amount determined by the costs incurred by the supplier to produce the goods and/or services purchased plus a stated percentage or fixed sum.

COST REDUCTION – The act of lowering the cost of goods or services by identifying and eliminating nonvalue-added cost or waste.

COST-REIMBURSEMENT CONTRACT – A family of pricing arrangements or contract types that provide for payment of allowable, allocable, and reasonable costs incurred in the performance of a contract to the extent that such costs are prescribed or permitted by the contract. These contracts establish an estimate of total cost for the purpose of obligating funds and establishing a ceiling that the contractor may not exceed without approval of the buyer.

Types of cost-reimbursement contracts include: (1) cost without fee, (2) cost-sharing, (3) cost-plus-incentive fee, (4) cost-plus-award fee, and (5) cost-plus-fixed fee.

COUNTERPURCHASE – A form of countertrade that occurs when a firm agrees to purchase a specific dollar volume of materials from a country in return for a sale made in that country.

COUNTERTRADE – A general term used for any type of transaction that requires, as a condition of the original sale, that goods be accepted either as a trade-balancing mechanism or as full or partial payment for the goods sold. Some form of countertrade frequently is used in international business transactions.

CREDIT MEMO – A method of correcting an over-charge, paying a trading rebate, or crediting the value of goods returned

CRITICAL-VALUE ANALYSIS – A modification of the ABC analysis concept in which the subjective value of criticalness, as opposed to the actual dollar value, is assigned to each inventory item.

CUMULATIVE DISCOUNT – A variation of a quantity discount that is based on the quantity purchased over a specified period of time, rather than being computed on the size of a single order placed at one time. This type of discount is commonly offered by suppliers as an incentive to a purchasing firm for continued or increased patronage.

CURRENT PRICE – The price currently being paid.

CUSTOM TARIFF – See Duties.

33

CUSTOMER – Any individual or process that receives or purchases the output(s) of a producer's services or goods, whether internal or external.

CYCLE COUNT (OR CONTINUOUS INVEN-TORY) – A physical stock checking system in which the inventory is divided into fifty-two equal groups, one of which is physically counted each week. Thus, the physical inventory operation goes on continuously without interrupting operations or storeroom activities.

CYCLE INVENTORY – See Cycle Stock.

CYCLE STOCK – The active portion of an inventory – i.e., that part of inventory which is depleted through regular withdrawals or use and is replenished through repetitive orders.

CYCLE TIME – In a purchasing context, the replenishment cycle represents the period of time required to order and make available the required stock (e.g., the time between receipt of the requisition and delivery of the material to the requisitioner). (See: order cycle)

CYCLE TIME MANAGEMENT (CTM) – The integration of all the activities of an organization from customer need to customer satisfaction under one operating philosophy which seeks to build better products or provide better services faster than its competitors.

D

d – The distance from the average ($\overline{X}$) in terms of the measurement.

d$_2$ – A divisor of $\overline{R}$ used to estimate the process standard deviation.

D$_3$ D$_4$ – Multipliers of $\overline{R}$ used to calculate the upper and lower control limits, respectively, for ranges.

DAILY WORK ORDER ACTIVITY – Shows how much regular and overtime was worked on each job the day before, and how much work still has to be done to complete it.

DAMAGES – In a purchasing context, damages are compensation of a specific value, determined by a court, to be paid for loss or injury suffered by one party to a contract as a result of the other contractual party's breach of the contract.

DEBIT MEMO – Document used to authorize the shipment of rejected material back to the supplier and create a debit entry in accounts payable.

DECENTRALIZED PURCHASING – When a firm approaches purchasing in a decentralized manner, individual departments (in a single-site organization) or location managers (in a multi-site organization) control the purchasing functions. There is no central purchasing department with specialized buying expertise in a single-site operation, although in a multi-site operation each plant may have its own purchasing department.

DECLARED VALUE – The practice of stating the value of goods being transported on the shipping document. Declared value can be used for the purpose of achieving a lower freight rate, obtaining insurance, etc.

DECOUPLING INVENTORY – Inventory retained to make possible the independent control of two operations, sometimes referred to as line-balancing stock.

DELINQUENT ORDER – A line item on the customer open order which has an original scheduled ship date prior to the current date.

DELIVER TO LOCATION – A location where you deliver goods you have previously received from a supplier to individual requestors.

DELIVERY – The internal delivery of items to requestors within your organization.

DELIVERY CYCLE – The actual time from the receipt of the customer order to the time of the shipment of the product.

DELIVERY ORDER – An order for supplies or services placed against an established contract. (See: release)

DELIVERY SCHEDULE – The required or agreed time or rate of delivery of goods or services purchased for future period.

DEMAND – A need for a particular product or component. The demand could come from any number of sources, i.e., customer order, forecast, interplant, branch warehouse, service part, or from manufacturing the next higher level.

DEMURRAGE – A fee charged by a carrier against a consignee, consignor, or other responsible party to compensate for the detention of the carrier's equipment (rail car, container, etc.) in excess of allowable free time for loading, unloading, reconsigning, or stopping in transit. The term is also used by suppliers of material delivered in a variety of returnable containers, such as gas cylinders, etc.

DEPENDENT DEMAND – Demand is considered dependent when it is directly related to or derived from the demand for other items or end products.

DEPRECIATION – An allocation of the original value of an asset against current income representing the declining value of the asset as a cost of that time period.

DESIGN FOR PRODUCIBILITY (DFP) – A process whereby quality is designed into the product and the process at the same time, thus guaranteeing that the product is producible and conforms to customer requirements.

DESIGN SPECIFICATION – A complete description of an item, including the composition of materials to be used in making the product, as well as size, shape, capacity, dimensions, tolerances, and sometimes method of treatment or manufacture. (See: specification)

DETAILED SCHEDULING – The actual assignment of target starting and/or completion dates to operations or groups of operations to show when these must be done if the manufacturing order is to be completed on time. These dates are used in the dispatching operation.

37

DIRECT COSTS – Variable costs which can be directly attributed to a particular job or operation.

DIRECT PRODUCT PROFITABILITY – Calculation of the net profit contribution attributable to a specific product or product line.

DIRECT RECEIPT – To receive items directly to the final destination (either the requestor or the point of use).

DIRECT SHIPMENT – The consignment of goods directly from the supplier to the buyer. Frequently used where a third party (distributor) acts as intermediary agent between supplier and buyer.

DISCOUNT – An allowance or deduction granted by the seller to the buyer, usually when certain stipulated conditions are met by the buyer, which reduces the cost of the goods purchased.

DISCRIMINATORY PRICE – A selling situation in which a supplier offers similar or identical items for sale, in identical quantities, at different prices to different buyers.

DISTRIBUTOR – A business that does not manufacture its own products but purchases and resells these products, usually maintaining an inventory of miscellaneous products.

DIVERSION – A carrier service that permits changing the destination or consignee of a shipment that is en route, either with or without an additional fee. This can be performed only at the request of the owner of the goods.

DOCK-TO-STOCK – That part of purchased goods and material that skips incoming inspection and goes directly into inventory after delivery.

DOCK-TO-WORK-IN-PROCESS (WIP) – Same as Dock-To-Stock except it is delivered to the point of use.

DOCUMENT – An object you need to describe or detail using standard or one-time notes.

DOCUMENT REFERENCE – A message that precisely identifies the document or part of document you want to describe using standard or one-time notes.

DOOR-TO-DOOR – The "through" transportation of a shipment of goods that goes from the consignor directly to the consignee.

DOWNTIME – The unproductive time when manufacturing processes are stopped, usually the result of equipment failure, setup, maintenance work, or material shortages.

DRAFT – A written order drawn by one party (drawer) ordering a second party (drawee) to pay a specified sum of money to a third party (payee).

DROP SHIPMENT – A distribution arrangement in which the seller serves as a selling agent by collecting orders but does not maintain inventory. The orders are sent to the manufacturer which ships directly to the customer.

DUE BILL – A bill levied by a government on the importation, exportation, or use and consumption of goods.

Glossary of Purchasing Terms

DUE DATE – The date at which purchased material or production on order is due to be available for use.

DUTY – A tax levied by a government on the importation, exportation, or use and consumption of goods. In the U.S., three types of duty rates may be used: *ad valorem* – a percentage of the appraised value, *specific* – a specified amount per unit, and *compound* – a combination of the ad valorem and specific rate approaches.

E

EARLY SUPPLIER INVOLVEMENT (ESI) – A practice that involves one or more selected suppliers with a buyer's product design team early in the specification development process. The objective is to use the supplier's expertise and experience in developing a product specification designed for effective and efficient manufacturability.

ECONOMIC ORDER QUANTITY (EOQ) – Determines the amount of product to be purchased or manufactured at one time in order to minimize the total cost involved, including the ordering costs (set-up of machines, writing orders, checking receipts, etc.) and carrying costs (costs of capital invested, insurance, taxes, space, obsolescence, and spoilage). The economic order quantity may be calculated from this equation:

$$EOQ = \sqrt{\frac{2 \cdot AS \cdot PC}{UC \cdot CC\%}}$$

where EOQ is the quantity ordered, AS is the annual usage, PC is the procurement cost, UC is the unit cost , and CC% is the carrying cost percentage.

ECONOMIC PRICE ADJUSTMENT – See Escalation.

ECONOMIES OF SCALE – The reduction in long-term average unit costs as the size (scale) of a firm or operation increases.

EFFICIENCY – The relationship between the planned resource requirements, such as labor or machine time, for a task(s) and the actual resource time charged to the task(s).

ELECTRONIC DATA INTERCHANGE (EDI) – The direct computer-to-computer exchange of business information in a standard format. Transaction documents, such as purchase orders, invoices, and shipping notices, are transmitted electronically and entered directly into a supplier's (or buyer's) computer or into a third-party network for processing.

EMPOWERMENT – The process by which an organization's leaders share management responsibility.

ENCUMBRANCE TYPE – An encumbrance category that allows you to track your expenditures according to your purchase approval process and better control your planned expenditures. You can set up separate encumbrance types for each stage in your purchasing cycle to track your spending at each level. Examples of encumbrance types are commitments (requisition encumbrances) and obligations (purchase order encumbrances).

ENGINEERING CHANGE – A revision to a product's configuration or specification.

ENGINEERING DRAWING – A blueprint that visually presents the dimensional characteristics of a part or assembly at some stage of manufacture.

ENTERPRISE RESOURCE PLANNING (ERP) – Working with a common database of enterprise wide information, all aspects of resource management are tied to the system. Starting with strategic and business planning, moving through operational planning and execution of the plans, information is collected at all phases and used as feedback for the entire cycle.

EQUIPMENT ID – Equipment identification number, name, location, etc.

ESCALATION – An amount or percentage by which a contract price may be adjusted if specified contingencies occur, such as changes in supplier's raw material or labor costs.

ESCALATOR CLAUSE – A contract clause generally permitting an increase in the price of goods or services in the event of certain outcomes, such as an increase in the supplier's raw materials or labor costs.

Escalation clauses in a contract typically also provide for de-escalation.

ESTABLISHED MARKET PRICE – A current price, generated in the usual course of business between buyers and sellers free to bargain, which can be substantiated from sources independent of the seller.

ETHICS – A system of moral principles or rules of conduct recognized (and prescribed in the case of a company or organization) as essential to a particular class of actions.

EX – A prefix used to denote the point at which title of goods passes; for example, ex-receiving dock at consignee's plant.

EXCEPTION – An occurrence of the specified condition found during a check. For example, testing for invoices on hold may find five invoices on hold, or none. Each invoice on hold is an exception.

EXCEPTION REPORTING – An integrated system of action sets that focuses attention on time-sensitive or critical information, shortens your reaction time, and provides faster exception distribution. Exception reporting communicates information by either electronic mail messages or paper reports.

EXEMPT COMMODITIES – Goods that are not subject to import duties, or specific goods which can be transported exempt of regulation by the Interstate Commerce Commission.

EXPECTED RECEIPTS REPORT – A printed report of all expected receipts for a time period and location you specify.

EXPEDITING – The "Prioritization" or "Tracing" of production or purchase orders which are needed in less than the normal lead time.

EXPEDITING FUNCTION – An inexact term sometimes used to describe a purchasing function whereby the status of purchase orders is constantly monitored to ensure that proper delivery schedules are met (also referred to as "follow-up"). This also may imply that constant pressure is maintained on a supplier to obtain punctual deliveries.

EXPEDITOR – A person whose primary duties are expediting.

EXPLOSION – An extension of a bill of material into the total of each of the components required to manufacture a given quantity of upper-level assembly or subassembly.

EXPRESS DELIVERY – An option that lets you deliver the entire quantity of a receipt without entering quantities for each shipment or distribution.

EXPRESS RECEIPT – A site option that lets you to receive an entire purchase order or blanket purchase agreement release with one keystroke.

EXPRESS REQUISITIONS – To create requisitions quickly from predefined requisition templates. You need to provide only quantities to create a requisition for commonly purchased items.

EXTERNAL DEMAND – See Independent Demand.

F

f – Frequency (how often each measurement occurred).

FABRICATION – A term used to distinguish manufacturing operations from assembly operations.

FACILITATOR – An individual who has been trained in the principles and tools of TQM so that he or she can support the activities of process improvement teams as they attempt to meet their goals.

FAILURE COSTS – Costs associated with products that do not conform to requirements. Activities in this area are typical of traditional quality methods and include scrap, rework, change orders, service and corrective action.

FAIR MARKET VALUE – The value of an item as determined by negotiation between purchasers and suppliers, which would be acceptable as a basis for a purchase and sale.

FEDERAL ACQUISITION REGULATION (FAR) – The acquisition uniform policy and procedure used by executive agencies of the federal government. FAR regulations are issued and maintained by the Department of Defense. FAR supersedes the Defense Acquisition Regulation (DAR).

FEE – In specified cost-reimbursement compensation arrangements, an agreed upon amount beyond the initial cost estimate, usually reflecting a variety of factors, including risk and services. The fee may be fixed initially (cost-plus-fixed-fee arrangement), or it may vary (cost-plus-incentive-fee or cost-plus-award-fee arrangement).

FILL RATE – The proportion of all stock requisitions that are filled from stock that is present on the shelf. The inverse of this is "stock-out rate," which is the percentage of orders for which there is no stock on the shelves and therefore the order cannot be filled (resulting in a "back order"). These measurements can be calculated for any time period; in some retail or distribution firms it might be computed daily or weekly.

FINISHED GOODS INVENTORIES – Inventories on which all manufacturing operations, including final test, have been completed. These may be either finished parts, like replacement parts, or finished products that have been authorized for transfer to the finished stock account. These products are now available for shipment to the customer either as end items or replacement parts.

FINITE LOADING – Conceptually the term means putting no more work into a factory than the factory can be expected to execute. The specific term usually refers to a computer technique that involves automatic shop priority revision in order to level load operation by operation. (Ant. infinite loading)

FIRM BID – Although many purchasers use the terms "bid," "proposal," and "quote" interchangeably in conversation, a "firm bid," "firm offer," or "firm quote" is thought of as a legal offer to sell, which can become a contract simply on acceptance by the buyer.

FIRM BIDDING – A policy by which purchasing firms notify suppliers that original bids must be final, and that revisions will not be permitted under any circumstances.

FIRM OFFER – See Firm Bid.

FIRST-IN-FIRST-OUT (FIFO) – A method of inventory valuation where the oldest inventory is the first to be used or sold, but has no necessary relationship to physical movement of the specified items.

FIRST-IN-STILL-HERE (FISH) – A company has received the product, but it was never shipped to the customer (i.e., normally obsolescent, slow moving inventory).

FISHBONE DIAGRAM – A brainstorming tool which shows causes and effects. The intent of this tool is to identify a problem and its possible causes and then to note the progress being made to eliminate those causes.

FIXED COST – A cost that is primarily related to a given time period and does not change due to production volume. Examples include rent, depreciation, and property taxes.

FIXED PRICE – A contract term which indicates that the price is set at a certain amount and is not subject to change, unless the purchaser requests a change in specifications, delivery, or terms.

FIXED-PRICE CONTRACTS – Refers to a family of pricing arrangements or contract types whose common discipline is a ceiling beyond which the buyer bears no responsibility for payment. Types include: (1) firm-fixed price, (2) fixed price with economic price adjustment/escalation, (3) fixed-price incentive, (4) fixed price with prospective price determination (rarely used), and (5) firm-fixed-price, level-of-effort term contracts (also rarely used).

FOLLOW-UP – See Expediting Function.

FORCE MAJEURE – Acts beyond the control of the party in question (e.g., acts of God or other disruptive conditions for which a supplier or a carrier cannot be held responsible).

FORECAST – A forecast is the extrapolation of the past into the future. It is an objective computation involving data as opposed to a prediction or subjective estimate incorporating management's anticipation of changes.

FOREIGN FREIGHT FORWARDER – A party that acts to arrange for foreign movement for shippers and consignees, distinct from domestic freight forwarders who take on different obligations.

FOREIGN TRADE ZONE – A site sanctioned by the Customs Service in which imported goods are exempted from customs duties until withdrawn for domestic sale or use. These zones are ideal for commercial warehouses or foreign production plants.

FORWARD BUYING – See Advance Buying.

FORWARD SCHEDULING – A scheduling technique when the scheduler proceeds from a known start date and computes the completion date for an order usually proceeding from the first operation to the last. (Ant. backward scheduling)

FOUR-WAY MATCHING – Purchasing performs four-way matching to verify that purchase order, receipt, inspection and invoice quantities match within tolerance.

FRAUD – Deceit, trickery, breach of confidence, or other illegal act used to gain some unfair or dishonest advantage.

FREE ALONG SIDE (F.A.S.) VESSEL – Under this arrangement, the supplier agrees to deliver the goods in proper condition along side the vessel, with the buyer assuming all subsequent risks and expenses after delivery to the pier.

FREE ON BOARD (F.O.B.) – The point at which title for goods transfers from seller to buyer. It also determines who is liable for transportation charges and who assumes the risk of lose of goods. The term "F.O.B." must be qualified by a name of location, such as shipping point, destination, name of a city, mill, warehouse, etc.

• **F.O.B. Destination, Freight Collect** means that title passes from the supplier to the buyer at the destination point, and that the freight charges are the responsibility of the purchaser. (The supplier owns the goods in transit and is responsible for filing loss and damage claims against the carrier, but the purchaser pays and bears the freight charges and files any overcharge claims.)

• **F.O.B. Destination, Freight Prepaid** means that title passes from the supplier to the buyer at the destination point, and that the freight charges are paid by the supplier. (The supplier pays and bears the freight charges, owns the goods in transit, and may file claims for overcharges, loss, damage, etc.)

• **F.O.B. Destination, Freight Prepaid and Charged** means that title passes at the destination point, and that the freight charges are paid by the supplier and added to the invoice. (The supplier pays the freight charges, owns the goods in transit, and files all claims for overcharges, loss, damages, etc. The purchaser bears the freight charges.)

• **F. O. B. Origin, Freight Allowed** means that purchaser obtains title where the shipment originates and is and is responsible for all claims against the carrier, but that the supplier pays for the freight charges.

•**F.O.B. Origin, Freight Collect** means that title passes to the buyer at the point of origin, and that the buyer must pay the freight charges. (The buyer owns the goods in transit and files all claims against the carrier.)

• **F.O.B. Origin, Freight Prepaid and Charged** means that title passes to the buyer at the point of origin, and that the freight charges are paid by the supplier and then collected from the purchaser by adding the amount of the freight charges to the invoice. (The supplier pays the freight charges and files claims for overcharges. The purchaser bears the freight charges, owns the goods in transit, and files claims for loss and damage with the carrier.)

FREEZE – You can freeze a purchase order after printing. By freezing a purchase order, you prevent anyone from adding new lines or changing the purchase order. You can continue to receive goods and be billed on already existing purchase order lines. The ability to continue receiving against the purchase order is the difference between freezing and cancelling.

FREIGHT BILL – The carrier's invoice for transportation charges applicable to a shipment.

FREIGHT BILL AUDIT – A critical review of freight bills to determine classification, rating, or extension, either by a third party or an inside auditor.

FREIGHT CLAIM – A claim against a carrier due to loss of, or damage to, goods transported by that carrier; also for erroneous rates and weights in assessment of freight charges.

FREIGHT CLASSIFICATION – See Class Freight Rate.

FREIGHT COLLECT – As it appears on the purchase order or contract, it indicates that the purchaser is responsible for freight charges directly to the carrier, regardless of the stated F.O.B. point. (See: free on board)

FREIGHT FORWARDER (DOMESTIC) – A carrier that collects small shipments from shippers (less-than truckload, less-than-carload, etc.) and consolidates them into larger shipments (truckloads, carloads, containers) for delivery to the consignee.

FUNCTIONAL CURRENCY – Currency you use to record transactions and maintain your accounting information within Purchasing. The functional currency is generally the currency you use to perform most of your company's business transactions. Also called base currency.

FUNDS AVAILABLE – The difference between your budget, less encumbrances of all types and actual expenditures.

FUTURES – Contracts for sale and delivery of commodities at a future time, made with the intention that no commodity be delivered or received immediately.

G

GATEWAY WORK CENTER – The first of a series of work centers through which the order is processed.

GLOBAL SOURCING – The procurement of goods or services outside the continental limits of the United States. In many firms, the term "global" infers the development of a longer term, planned continuing relationship with international suppliers.

GOODWILL – One of the intangible values beyond its net worth that a business acquires from suppliers and customers. It is promoted by granting more business as a reward for good service, sharing plans and forecasts, working together to solve problems, mutual research and development, etc.

GRANDFATHER CLAUSE – A contractual or legal provision that protects the existing interests of affected parties.

GROSS REQUIREMENTS – The total of independent and dependent demand for a component or an assembly prior to the netting of inventory and scheduled receipts.

GUARANTEE – See Warranty.

H

HANDLING COST – The cost involved in handling materials.

HAND-TO-MOUTH BUYING – Purchasing over a short period of time to meet only immediate, short-term requirements.

HAZARD CLASS – A category of hazardous materials. Most hazardous materials belong to only one hazard class. Some materials belong to more than one hazard class and some materials do not belong to any. If a material belongs to more than one hazard class, you should list these classes in a specific order.

HEDGING – A "futures" purchase or sale entered into for the purpose of balancing a sale or purchase already made, or under contract, in order to offset the effect of potential market price fluctuations. (See: futures)

HOLDING COST – See Inventory Holding Cost.

HUNDREDWEIGHT (CWT) – A common unit of weight used in transportation; 100 pounds.

I

IDLE TIME –See Down Time.

IMPLIED WARRANTY OF FITNESS FOR A PARTICULAR PURPOSE – A warranty that involves the purchaser asking the supplier for advice in the selection of a particular item. The purchaser can expect that the item recommended for purchase will fit the specified application.

INACTIVE/EXCESS INVENTORY – Designates the stocks that are in excess of contemplated consumption within planning period, typically 12 – 24 months.

INCOTERMS – International rules for the interpretation of terms used in foreign trade contracts, recognized by businesses worldwide. (e.g., INCOTERMS include such items as F.A.S., C.I.F., C&F, F.O.B., etc.)

INCREMENTAL FUNDING – The obligation of funds to a contract (which contains a total price or estimated cost) in periodic installments as the work progresses, rather than in a lump sum.

INDEFINITE DELIVERY CONTRACTS – There are three types of indefinite-delivery or "term"-type contracts: (1) definite quantity-indefinite delivery contracts, (2) indefinite quantity-definite delivery contracts, and (3) requirements contracts. The appropriate type of indefinite delivery-type contract may be used when the exact times and/or quantities of future deliveries are not known at the time of contract award.

INDEPENDENT CONTRACTOR – The following elements are essential to establish the relationship of an independent contractor to its client, as contrasted with the relationship of an agent to its principal. An independent contractor must: (1) exercise independent judgment as to the means used to accomplish the result; (2) be free from control or orders from any other person; and (3) be responsible only under the contract with the client for the result obtained.

INDEPENDENT DEMAND – Demand unrelated to the demands for other items or end items produced by the firm. It is also known as external demand.

INDEX NUMBERS – Ratios, usually expressed as percentages, indicating changes in values, quantities, or prices. Typically, the changes are measured over time, each item being compared with a corresponding figure from some selected base period.

INDIRECT COSTS – Costs which cannot be conveniently charged to a particular job or operation.

INDIRECT LABOR – Workers required to support production without being related to a specific product or assembly line.

INDIRECT MATERIALS – Materials which become part of the final product but are used in such small quantities that their cost is not applied directly to the product. Instead the cost becomes part of manufacturing supplies or overhead costs.

INFINITE LOADING – The practice of calculating load on a resource without any consideration for capacity limitations.

INPUT/OUTPUT CONTROL – A technique whereby actual input and actual output of a work center are monitored and compared with planned input and planned output.

INSPECTION – See Quality Inspection.

INTEGRATED SUPPLY – A special type of partnering arrangement usually developed between a purchaser and a distributor on an intermediate to long-term basis. The objective of an integrated supply relationship is to minimize, for both buyer and supplier, the labor and expense involved in acquisition and possession of maintenance, repair and operating (MRO) products – items that are repetitive, generic, high-transaction, and have a low unit cost.

INTERMODAL FREIGHT SHIPMENTS – Transportation shipments involving more than one mode, e.g., rail-motor, motor-air, rail-water, etc.

INTERNAL DEMAND – See Dependent Demand.

INTERNATIONAL FEDERATION OF PURCHASING/MATERIALS MANAGEMENT (IFPMM) – An international purchasing organization which has as its objective fostering cooperation, education, and research in purchasing on a worldwide basis among its member national associations.

INTEROPERATION TIME – The elapsed time between the completion of an operation at one work center and the start of work on that order at the next work center.

INTERSTATE COMMERCE COMMISSION (ICC) – An independent regulatory agency that implements federal economic regulations on certain aspects of operations of railroads, motor carriers, pipelines, domestic water carriers, domestic freight forwarders, and brokers. Although the transportation industry has been substantially deregulated since the late 1970s, the ICC continues to operate, and certain economic regulations exist in today's transportation environment.

IN-TRANSIT PRIVILEGES – These special privileges give rail shippers (buyers and sellers) the right to stop a shipment en route, unload it, perform certain processing operations on the material, reload the processed material, and continue the shipment at the original rate plus a modest additional charge.

INVENTORY – Items which are in a stocking location or work-in-process location. Inventories usually consist of finished goods, work-in-process, and purchased materials.

INVENTORY CONTROL – The activities and techniques of maintaining the stock of items at desired levels, whether they be raw materials, work-in-process, or finished goods.

INVENTORY HOLDING (CARRYING) COST – The cost of keeping inventory on hand, including the opportunity cost of invested funds, storage and handling costs, taxes, insurance, shrinkage, and obsolescence risk costs. Firms usually state an item's holding cost per time period as a percentage of the item's value, typically between 20 and 40 percent per year.

INVENTORY IN TRANSIT – Physical inventory en route aboard a carrier. The term is also used to mean the capital costs of materials, parts, and finished goods en route aboard a carrier. This cost is commonly computed by multiplying the opportunity cost rate by the value of the inventory and by the percentage of time (annualized) the goods are en route, plus the cost of the material itself.

INVENTORY INVESTMENT – The total cost of all inventory.

INVENTORY ITEM – Items that you stock in inventory. You control inventory for inventory items by quantity and value. Typically, the inventory item remains an asset until you consume it. You recognize the cost of an inventory item as an expense when you consume it or sell it. You generally value the inventory for an item by multiplying the item standard cost by the quantity on hand.

INVENTORY ORDERING COST – The total cost of generating and processing an order and its related paper work.

INVENTORY POLICY – A statement of philosophy which directs the management of inventory upon which procedures will be established.

INVENTORY POSITION – A measure of an inventory item's ability to satisfy future demand, considering scheduled receipts and on-hand inventory.

INVENTORY SHRINKAGE – Losses resulting from scrap, deterioration, pilferage, etc.

INVENTORY TRANSACTION – A record of material movement. The basic information for a transaction includes the item number, the quantity moved, the transaction amount, and the date. (See: material transaction)

INVENTORY TURNOVER – The number of times that the inventory dollar value is consumed by cost of goods sold during the year. The way to compute inventory turnover is to divide the cost of goods sold by the average inventory value.

INVENTORY USAGE – The amount of inventory used or consumed over a period of time.

INVENTORY VALUATION – The value of the inventory which can be calculated at either its cost or its market value. Because inventory value can change with time, some recognition must be taken of the age distribution of inventory. Therefore, the cost value of inventory, under accounting practice, is usually computed on a first-in-first-out (FIFO), last-in-first-out (LIFO) basis.

INVENTORY WRITE-OFF – A deduction of inventory dollars from the financial statement because the inventory is no longer saleable or because of shrinkage.

INVESTMENT RECOVERY – A systematic, centralized organizational effort to manage the surplus equipment/material and scrap recovery/marketing/ disposition activities in a manner that recovers as much of the original capital investment as possible.

INVITATION FOR BIDS – The request made to potential suppliers for a firm bid on goods or services to be purchased. This term is also used in government purchasing to refer to the solicitation document used in sealed bidding and in the second step of two-step bidding.

INVOICE – A bill for goods or services being purchased that includes pertinent information with respect to the quantity, price, terms, nature of delivery, etc.

INVOICE PRICE VARIANCE – The difference between the purchase order price for an item and the actual invoice price multiplied by the quantity invoiced. Payables records this variance after matching the invoice to the purchase order. Typically, the price variance is small since the price the supplier charges you for an item should be the one you negotiated on your purchase order.

ISO 9000 – A comprehensive set of requirements regarding a documented quality system developed by the International Standards Organization.

ISSUE CYCLE – The time required to complete the cycle of material issues. It includes generating a requisition, pulling the material from an inventory location and moving it to its destination.

ITEM – Any unique manufactured or purchased part or assembly, such as finished product, assembly, subassembly, component, or raw material.

ITEM MASTER FILE – A computer file that contains identifying and descriptive data, control values, and data on inventory status, requirements, and planned orders. There is normally one record in this file for each stock keeping unit.

J

JOB – A category of personnel in your organization. Examples of a typical job include Vice President, Buyer, and Manager. (See: position)

JOINT VENTURE – A business venture or investment undertaken by two or more firms.

JUST-IN-TIME (J.I.T.) – A philosophy that promotes the manufacturing of the right product, in the right quantities, on time, at the lowest total cost to meet customer requirements.

K

k – The number of subgroups to calculate $\bar{\bar{X}}$ and $\bar{R}$.

KANBAN SYSTEM – A system of production flow control that utilizes Kanban cards to "pull" in-process inventories through a manufacturing process, where items are called for only as they are needed in the next step of the production process.

KIT – The components of an assembly that have been pulled from stock and readied for movement to the assembly area.

KITTING – The process of removing components of an assembly from the stockroom and sending them to the assembly floor as a kit of parts.

KNOCKED DOWN (KD) – Disassembled goods for the purpose of reducing the cube space of the shipment for transportation and storage.

L

LABOR-HOUR CONTRACTS – A labor-hour contract is a variation of the time-and-materials contract, differing only in that materials are not supplied by the contractor.

LABOR LOADING – The process of applying expected labor requirements against the capacity for that labor.

LABOR PRODUCTIVITY – The rate of output of a worker or group of workers, per unit of time, compared to an established standard or rate of output.

LABOR TIMESHEETS – For a given employee, enter hours worked on various work orders, regular, overtime, and call-in hours.

LAST-IN-FIRST-OUT (LIFO) – A method of inventory valuation where the most recently received inventory is the first to be used or sold, but has no necessary relationship to physical movement of specified items.

LATEST START – The latest an operation can start, take the normal processing lead time and still meet the planned need date.

LCL – Lower Control Limit.

LCL$_R$ – Lower Control Limit for Ranges.

$$= D_3\overline{R}$$

LCL$_{\overline{X}}$ – Lower Control Limit for Averages.

$$= X - A_2\overline{R}$$

LEAD TIME – A period of time required to perform an activity, such as the procurement of materials and/or the production of products from manufacturing facility.

LEARNING CURVE – Sometimes called the "improvement curve," the learning curve depicts an empirical relationship between the number of units produced and the number of labor hours required to produce them. The curve is most applicable to the production of repetitively produced complex products. Buyers can use the learning curve to analyze the effects of learning on unit costs, and production managers can use it to determine manpower and scheduling requirements. There are two types of learning curves – the cumulative average curve and the unit curve.

LEASE – Acquisition of real and personal property by means of a contract in which the lessor conveys to the lessee the use of the property in return for a specified rent or other compensation.

LEASE-OR-BUY DECISION – The decision concerning whether to contract for the possession and use of an asset owned by another party for a period of time, in return for lease payments, as opposed to purchasing the asset.

LEGAL TENDER – Money (currency or coin) declared by a government to be legal in the payment of a debt or duty.

LESS-THAN-CARLOAD (L.C.L.) – A shipment which is less than the amount required to be eligible for carload rates.

LESS-THAN-TRUCKLOAD (L.T.L.) – A shipment which is less than the amount required to be eligible for truckload rates.

LETTER CONTRACT – A preliminary written contractual instrument that authorizes the contractor to begin immediately performing the manufacturing or services requested. The letter contract typically is followed by a definitive contract document.

LETTER OF CREDIT – An international business document that assures the seller that payment will be made by the bank issuing the letter of credit upon fulfillment of the sales agreement.

LETTER OF INTENT – A preliminary contractual arrangement used to enter into preliminary agreements where further negotiation is required, pending a definitive contract.

LIEN – A legal claim on property for the purpose of satisfying a debt.

LIFE-CYCLE COSTING – A cost-analysis tool which incorporates not only the purchase price of a piece of equipment, but all operating and related costs over the life of the item, including maintenance, down time, energy costs, etc., as well as salvage value.

LIMITING OPERATION – In a series of operations with no alternative routings, the capacity of the total system can be no greater than the operation with the least capacity. As long as this limiting condition exists, the total system can be effectively scheduled by simply scheduling the limiting operation. (Syn. bottleneck)

LINE TYPE – Determines whether a purchasing document line is for goods, services, or any other type that you define. The line type also determines whether the document line is based on price and quantity or on amount.

LIQUIDATED DAMAGES – A sum agreed upon between the parties to a contract, to be paid as ascertained damages by the party that breaches the contract, if a breach occurs

LOAD – This is the amount of scheduled work ahead of a manufacturing facility, usually expressed in terms of hours of work units or production.

LOAD LEVELING – Spreading orders out in time or rescheduling operations so that the amount of work to be done in the time periods tends to be distributed evenly. (Ant. finite loading)

LOAD PROFILE – A display of future capacity requirements based on planned and released orders over a given span of time. (Syn. load projection)

LOAD PROJECTION – See Load Profile.

LOADING ALLOWANCE – A reduced rate or refund offered to shippers and/or consignees who load and/or unload the shipment.

LOGISTICS – The process of planning, implementing, and controlling the efficient, cost-effective flow and storage of raw materials, in-process inventory, finished goods, and related information from point of origin to point of consumption for the purpose of conforming to customer requirements.

LONG-TERM CONTRACTING – A decision to contract with a particular supplier over an extended period of time.

LOT NUMBER – A unique identification assigned to a quantity of material to be procured or manufactured for the purpose of traceability.

LOT SIZES – The amount of a particular item that is ordered from or produced by a manufacturing operation. (Syn. order quantity)

LSL – The lower engineering specification limit.

LUMP SUM – A lot price or a fixed-total price paid in one sum.

M

MRO – Maintenance, repair, and operating supplies that are consumed in the operations process, but which do not become part of the product of the operation (e.g., soap, lubricating oil, machine repair parts, office supplies, etc.).

MACHINE LOAD – The total work in standard hours waiting to be processed on a machine.

MAKE-OR-BUY DECISION – The act of deciding whether to produce an item in-house or buy it from an outside supplier.

MAKE-TO-ORDER PRODUCT – The end item is finished after receipt of a customer order. Frequently long lead time components are forecast prior to the order arriving so as to reduce the delivery time to the customer. Where options or other subassemblies are stocked prior to customer orders arriving, the term "assemble-to-order" is frequently used.

MAKE-TO-STOCK PRODUCT – The end item is manufactured to and shipped from finished goods, "off the shelf."

MANIFEST – An itemization of the items shipped, plus related details. Often the manifest is simply a copy of the freight bill.

MANUFACTURER'S REPRESENTATIVE – A manufacturer's representative is an independent entrepreneur who functions as a sales agent for one or more manufacturers. Rep's typically do not buy the products they sell, rarely carry inventory, and sell at prices dictated by the manufacturer.

MANUFACTURING LEAD TIME – The total time required to manufacture an item. Included here are order preparation time, queue time, set-up time, run time, move time, inspection, etc.

MANUFACTURING ORDER – A document or group of documents conveying authority for the manufacture of specified parts or products in specified quantities.

MANUFACTURING PROCESS – The series of activities performed upon material to convert it from raw or semifinished state to a state of further completion and of increased value.

MANUFACTURING RESOURCE PLANNING (MRP II) – A method for the effective planning of all the resources of a manufacturing company. Ideally, it addresses operational planning in units, financial planning in dollars, and has a simulation capability to answer "what if" questions. It is made up of a variety of functions, each linked together: Business Planning, Production Planning, Master Production Scheduling, Material Requirements Planning (MRP I), Capacity Requirements Planning, and the execution systems for capacity and priority. Outputs from these systems are integrated with financial reports such as the business plan, purchase commitment report, shipping budget, inventory projections in dollars, etc. Manufacturing Resource Planning (MRP II) is a direct outgrowth and extension of Material Requirements Planning (MRP I).

MARKET GRADE – A product that is of "fair, average quality." This means that the item meets the standards of the trade and that its quality is appropriate for ordinary use; it is used in applying the implied warranty of merchantability.

Glossary of Purchasing Terms

MARKET SHARE – The actual portion of available customer demand that a company achieves.

MASTER FILE – A main reference file of information such as bills of material or routing files.

MASTER PRODUCTION SCHEDULE (MPS) – It represents what the company plans to produce expressed in specific configurations, quantities, and dates.

MATERIAL – Any commodity used directly or indirectly in producing a product, raw materials, component parts, subassemblies, supplies, etc.

MATERIAL REQUIREMENTS PLANNING (MRP I) – Typically, a computer program that calculates required quantities and dates for items based on a statement of end item demand. Bills of material, lead times, etc. are used in these calculations

MATERIALS MANAGEMENT – A term to describe the grouping of management functions related to the complete cycle of material flow, from the purchase and internal control of production materials to the planning and control of work-in-process to warehousing, shipping and distribution of the finished product.

MINIMUM REORDER POINT – A predetermined inventory level that triggers a need to place an order. This minimum level (considering safety stock) provides inventory to meet anticipated demand during the time it takes to receive the order.

MINORITY BUSINESS ENTERPRISE (MBE) – Any legal entity, organized to engage in commercial transaction, that is at least fifty-one percent owned and controlled by one or more minority persons.

MOST-FAVORED-CUSTOMER CLAUSE – A price protection clause in a contract which specifies that the supplier will not offer a lower price to other buyers unless also applicable to said contract.

MOVE TIME – See Transit Time.

MULTIPLE DISCOUNT – A trade discount structured as a sequence of individual discounts. (See: trade discount)

MULTI-SOURCE – An option that lets a buyer distribute the quantity of a single requisition line to several suppliers whenever the buyer wants to purchase the requisition line item from more than one supplier.

MUTUAL ASSENT – Consists of an offer made by one party and the unconditional acceptance of that offer by another party.

N

n – Sample size.

NATIONAL CONTRACT – A negotiated agreement between a purchaser and a supplier which typically extends the contract terms and discounts to all company locations.

NEGOTIATION – The process by which a purchasing professional and a supplier agree to terms and conditions surrounding the purchase of an item.

NEGOTIATION TEAM – A team constituted for the purpose of conducting a specific negotiation. Team members typically represent the functional areas to be addressed in the negotiation process; the purchasing member usually chairs the team.

NET CHANGE MRP – An approach in which the material requirements plan requires a change in requirements, open order or inventory status, or engineering usage. A partial explosion is made only for those parts affected by the change.

NET REQUIREMENTS – Requirements for a part or an assembly are derived as a result of netting gross requirements against inventory on hand and the scheduled receipts.

NOT OTHERWISE SPECIFIED (N.O.S.) – A classification indicating commodities not completely identified.

NOTE NAME – A name that uniquely identifies a standard or one-time note. You use note names to locate a note you want to use or copy on a document.

NUMERIC NUMBER TYPE – An option for numbering documents, employees, and vendors where assigned numbers contain only numbers.

O

OBLIGATION – A monetary liability of the buyer, limited in amount to the legal liability of the buyer at the time of record. Contract and purchase orders represent monetary obligation of a buyer to a supplier.

OFFER – An offer is an invitation to "come do business with me on these terms." It is a promise made to the other party that if the terms proposed are satisfactory there will be a contract. It is, in fact, a legal commitment to the other party to form a contract if that person agrees. (See: firm bid)

OFFSET – A form of countertrade similar to counterpurchase, in which a supplier selling to a foreign firm agrees to purchase a certain quantity of materials from the country it supplies. The primary difference is that the supplier can fulfill its obligation by purchasing from any company in the country it supplies.

OFFSHORE – Being or operating out of domestic boundaries.

OH SHOOT! WE'RE OUT! (OSWO) – A total out of stock situation based on surprise.

ON HAND – The balance shown in perpetual inventory records as being physically present at a stocking location.

ON ORDER – The stock on order is the quantity represented by the total of all outstanding replenishment orders. The on order balance increases when a new order is released, and it decreases when material is received to fill an order or when an order is canceled.

ON-TIME DELIVERY – Delivery of material or product on time, 100% of the time. On time is defined as a window in which both early and late deliveries are unacceptable.

ONE-TIME ITEM – An item you want to order but do not want to maintain in the Define Items form. You define a one-time item when you create a requisition or purchase order. You can report or query on a one-time item by specifying the corresponding item class.

ONE-TIME NOTE – A long note that you define as you create the document where you want the note to appear.

ONE TOUCH CHANGEOVER (OTC) – A set-up reduction method which aims to reduce a changeover to one action with no setting, testing, resetting, and retesting before a good part is made.

OPEN-END ORDER – This type of order generally specifies all terms except quantity. Shipments are made against the buyer's release orders per the contract; similar to a blanket order.

OPEN-MARKET PRICE – A price quoted publicly on a daily or weekly basis.

OPEN ORDER – The quantity of a purchase order, sales order, or factory order yet to be satisfied.

OPERATION DURATION – The time required for an operation to be set up and run.

OPERATION SPLITTING – The processing of a lot of material on two similar machines. This usually increases cost as two set-ups are required.

OPTION – 1. A choice or feature offered to customers for customizing the end product. The customer must select from one of the available choices.

2. A unilateral right in a contract, by means of which, for a specified time, the buyer may elect to purchase additional supplies or services called for in the contract, or may elect to extend the term of the contract.

ORDER – See Bid, Contract, Open-End Order, Purchase Order.

ORDER CYCLE – The time that elapses from placement of an order to receipt of the order, including time for order transmittal, processing, preparation, and shipping.

ORDER POINT – When the inventory level of an item (stock on hand plus on order) falls to or below the order point, action is taken to replenish the stock.

ORDERING COSTS – See Inventory Ordering Costs or Acquisition Costs.

ORIGINAL EQUIPMENT MANUFACTURER (OEM) – A purchaser who acquires materials or components for incorporation into production of another product. "OEM parts" refer to spare parts made by the original manufacturer (e.g., a Ford part vs. a Mopar part).

OUTSIDE OPERATION – An operation that contains outside resources and possibly internal resources as well.

OUTSIDE PROCESSING – Performing work on a discrete job or repetitive schedule using resources provided by a supplier.

OUTSIDE PROCESSING ITEM – An item you include on a purchase order line to purchase supplier services as part of your assembly build process. This item can be the assembly itself or a non-stocked item which represents the service performed on the assembly.

OUTSIDE RESOURCE – A resource supplied by a suppier that you include in your routings, such as supplier supplied labor or service. This includes both purchase order (PO) move and purchase order (PO) receipt resources.

OUTSOURCING – A version of the make-or-buy decision in which a firm elects to purchase an item that previously was made in-house; commonly utilized for services.

OVER, SHORT, AND DAMAGE REPORT – A report issued by a freight agent which indicates discrepancies between the bill of lading and freight on hand.

OVERHEAD – Costs incurred in the operation of a business that cannot be directly related to the individual products or services produced.

OVERHEAD PERCENTAGE – The percentage applied to a labor cost to calculate the overhead cost of performing work in that work center.

OVERLAPPING – The "overlapping" of successive operations, whereby the completed portion of a job lot at one work center is processed at one or more succeeding work centers before the pieces left behind are finished at the preceding work center(s).

OVERLOAD – When the total work in standard hours outstanding at a machine exceeds that machine's capacity.

OVER-RUN – The quantity received from manufacturing or a supplier that is in excess of the quantity ordered.

OVERTIME – Work beyond normal established working hours which usually requires that a premium be paid to the workers.

P

p – Proportion or fraction rejected.

$\bar{p}$ – Average fraction rejected.

PACKING SLIP – A document which itemizes in detail the contents of a particular package or shipment.

PALLET – A platform device used for moving and/or storing goods.

PARADIGM – Those rules and regulations that govern and limit our way of thinking.

PARAMETER – A variable you use to restrict information in a report, or determine the form of a report. For example, you may want to limit your report to the current month or display information by supplier number instead of supplier name.

PARETO'S LAW – A concept developed by Pareto, an Italian economist, which simply says that a small percentage of a group account for the largest fraction of the cost.

PAR-STOCK SYSTEM – See Base-Stock System.

PART – Refers to an item which is used as a component, an assembly, or subassembly.

PART NUMBER – A number which serves to uniquely identify a component, product, or raw material.

PARTIAL ORDER – Any shipment received or shipped which is less than the amount ordered.

PARTIAL PAYMENT – A method of payment for accepted supplies and services that are only a part of the contract requirements.

PARTNERING – See Supplier Partnership.

PARTS PER MILLION (PPM) – A measure of quantity that may be used in a quality specification, whereby defective parts must not exceed a specified number of parts per million parts supplied; a ratio of number of failures to number of parts supplied.

PAST DUE – An order that has not been completed on time.

PAYMENT DISCOUNT – See Cash Discount.

PENALTY CLAUSE – An inexact term meaning a clause in a contract that specifies the sum of money due in case of contractual default. Such a clause is in reality a liquidated damages clause and cannot specify compensation in excess of the actual injury sustained by the injured firm. Courts will not enforce a "penalty" on the defaulting party. (See: liquidated damages)

PER DIEM – Although this term literally means "per day," it is used in various ways to take on more specific meanings. For example, from a transportation perspective, a per diem charge is the daily rate for use of rail cars of one railroad by another railroad.

PERFORMANCE BOND – See Bond.

PERFORMANCE MEASUREMENT – A management technique for evaluating the performance of a particular function or person. (See: benchmark)

PERFORMANCE SPECIFICATION – A specification that details the functional performance criteria required for a particular material or product (as opposed to a design specification, which prescribes in detail the design characteristics and manufacturing methodology for the material or product).

PERIOD EXPENSE – An expense that you record in the period it occurs. An expense is typically a debit.

PERIODIC-REVIEW SYSTEM – A "fixed-order interval" inventory control system in which an item's inventory position is reviewed on a scheduled periodic basis, rather than continuously. An order is placed at the end of each review, and the order quantity usually varies. This system is different from a "fixed-order quantity" system in which the order quantity typically is fixed and the time between orders varies.

PERPETUAL-INVENTORY SYSTEM – An inventory control record system which requires immediate recording of transactions (receipts and withdrawals) for each item carried in inventory. If posted accurately, the inventory records are up to date and should agree with the actual stock count in the warehouse.

PETTY CASH PURCHASE – A method of purchasing low-value items from a firm's petty cash system. This is often combined with a C.O.D. approach.

PICKING – The process of "picking" items from warehouse stock; assembling the items required to fill an order, usually performed with the assistance of a picking list.

PICKUP AND DELIVERY (P.U. & D.) – Transport service from the shipper's dock to the consignee's dock.

PIECE PARTS – Consists of individual items in inventory at the entry level in manufacturing. For example, bolts and washers.

PIGGYBACK INVENTORY – See Trailer-on-Flat-car.

PIPELINE INVENTORY – Materials inventory in transit from the supplier to the buyer.

PLANNED ORDER – A suggested order quantity and due date created by Material Requirements Planning (MRP I) processing, when it encounters net requirements. Planned orders are created by the computer, exist only within the computer, and may be changed or deleted by the computer during subsequent Material Requirements Planning (MRP I) processing if conditions change. Planned orders at one level will be exploded into gross requirements for components at the next lower level. Planned orders also serve as input to capacity requirements planning, along with released orders, to show the total capacity requirements in future time periods.

PLANNED ORDER RELEASE (POR) – A planned authorization for a supplier to release (to ship) material against an existing contract. As used in Material Requirements Planning (MRP I) system operation, the POR indicates when a release for a specified quantity of an item is to be issued; the release date is the planned receipt date minus the lead time.

PLANNED PURCHASE ORDER – A type of purchase order you issue before you order actual delivery of goods and services for specific dates and locations. You normally enter a planned purchase order to specify items you want to order and when you want delivery of the items. You later enter a shipment release against the planned purchase order when you actually want to order the items.

PLANNING HORIZON – In a Material Requirements Planning (MRP I) system, the planning horizon is the span of time from the current to some future date for which material plans are generated. This must cover at least the cumulative purchasing and manufacturing lead time, and usually is quite a bit longer.

POINT OF ORIGIN – The location where a transportation company receives a shipment from the shipper.

POSITION – A specific function within a job category. Examples of typical positions associated with the Vice President job include: Vice President of Manufacturing, Vice President of Engineering, and Vice President of Sales. (See: job)

POSITION HIERARCHY – A structure of positions used to define management line reporting and control access to employee information.

PREPAID – A term denoting that charges have been or are to be paid by the shipper.

PRESURVEY – A survey of a supplier which is used to determine whether they will continue in the Supplier Certification process. Typically, this is a mailed survey.

PREVENTION COSTS – Costs associated with ensuring that products conform to requirements. Activities in this area are typical of Total Quality Management methods and include supplier qualification, process control, zero-defects and preventive maintenance.

PREVENTIVE MAINTENANCE – A program of maintenance which seeks, through statistical methods, to make routine repairs or maintenance before a breakdown occurs.

PRICE – The amount of money exchanged for a good or service between a supplier and customer.

PRICE ANALYSIS – Price analysis is the examination of a supplier's price proposal (bid) by comparison with reasonable benchmarks, without examination and evaluation of the separate elements of cost and profit making up the price.

PRICE BREAK LINE – Supplier pricing information for an item or purchasing category on a quotation. The price you enter on a price break line depends on the quantity you order from your supplier. Usually, suppliers provide you with price break line structures to indicate the price you would pay for an item depending on the quantity you order. Generally, the more you order, the less expensive your unit price. Also, depending on the quantity you order, a supplier may provide you with different purchase conditions, such as advantageous payment or freight terms when you buy in large quantities.

PRICE INDEX – A number, usually a percentage, expressing the relation of the actual price of a commodity at a given point in time to its price during a specified base period. This information can be used to chart price level changes.

PRICE PREVAILING AT THE DATE OF SHIP-MENT – An agreement between the purchaser and the supplier that the price of the goods ordered will be based on the price on the day of shipment.

PRICE PROTECTION – An agreement by a supplier with a customer to grant the purchaser a price which the supplier established should the price increase prior to shipment.

PRICE SCHEDULE – The list of prices applying to varying quantities or types of goods.

PRIME COSTS – Direct costs of material and labor; does not include general sales and administrative costs.

PRIORITY – In a general sense, refers to the relative importance of jobs, i.e., which jobs should be worked on and when.

PRIORITY CONTROL – Control with the purpose of ensuring planned priorities are followed by the shop.

PRIORITY PLANNING – Assigning priorities to jobs outstanding at each work center so manufacturing targets can be met.

PRIVATE CARRIER – A carrier that owns or leases vehicles and provides transportation services for the firm which owns it.

PROCEDURE MANUAL – A formal organization and indexing of a firm's policies and practices.

PROCEDURES – Definitions of approved methods of operation.

PROCESS – An interdependent set of work tasks that together meet some need, whether service or manufacturing related.

PROCESS SHEET – Detailed manufacturing instructions issued to the shop. The instructions may include speeds, feeds, tools, fixtures, machines, and sketches of set-ups and semifinished dimensions (i.e. routing).

PROCESS TIME – The time during which the material is being changed, whether it is a machining operation or a hand assembly.

PROCUREMENT – Purchasing activities that typically include specifications development, value analysis, supplier market research, negotiation, buying activities, contract administration, and perhaps inventory control, traffic, receiving, and stores.

PROCUREMENT LEAD TIME – The time required by the buyer to select a supplier and to place and obtain a commitment for specific quantities of material at specified times.

PRODUCT – Any commodity produced for sale.

PRODUCT MIX – The combination of individual product types and the volume produced that make up the total production volume. Changes in the product mix can mean drastic changes in the manufacturing requirements for labor and material.

PRODUCT STRUCTURE – The way components go into a product during its manufacture. A typical product structure would show, for example, raw material being converted into fabricated components, components being put together to make subassemblies, subassemblies going into assemblies, etc.

PRODUCTION CONTROL – The function of directing or regulating the movement of goods through the entire manufacturing cycle from the requisitioning of raw materials to the delivery of finished product.

PRODUCTION CYCLE – The lead time to produce a product.

PRODUCTION MATERIAL – Any material used in the manufacturing process.

PRODUCTION RATES – The quantity of production usually expressed in units, hours. Expressed by a unit of time.

PRODUCTION REPORT – A formal, written statement giving information on the output of an organization for a specified period.

PRODUCTION SCHEDULE – A plan which authorizes the plant to manufacture a certain quantity of a specific item.

PROFIT – Profit is generally characterized as the basic motive of a business enterprise. In contract pricing, profit represents a projected or known monetary residual realized by a seller after the deduction of all costs (direct and indirect) from the selling price of the item.

PRO FORMA INVOICE – A document prepared in advance of a sale to provide evidence of the final form and amount of invoice.

PROGRESS PAYMENTS – Payments arranged in connection with purchase transactions requiring periodic payments in advance of delivery.

PROMISSORY NOTE – A written promise from one party to another to pay a specific sum of money at a specific time to the bearer or other designated party.

PROSPECTIVE PRICING – A pricing decision made in advance of performance, based on an analysis of comparative prices, cost estimates, past costs, or combinations of such considerations.

PUBLIC SECTOR PURCHASING – The purchasing function as carried out by governmental agencies.

PUBLIC WAREHOUSE – A place for storage of goods managed by a firm that offers the storage service to the public for a fee.

PURCHASE CYCLE TIME – The time from when a purchase order is placed to the time the product is received on site.

PURCHASE ORDER (PO) – 1. The purchaser's document used to formalize a purchase transaction with a supplier.

2. A type of purchase order you issue when you request delivery of goods or services for specific dates and locations. You can order multiple items for each planned or standard purchase order. Each purchase order line can have multiple shipments and you can distribute each shipment across multiple accounts. (See: standard purchase order and planned purchase order)

PURCHASE ORDER (PO) DRAFT – See Blank-Check Purchase Order.

PURCHASE ORDER (PO) MOVE RESOURCE – An outside resource that is automatically charged upon receipt of a purchase order. PO move resources also automatically initiate shop floor move transactions upon receipt.

PURCHASE ORDER (PO) RECEIPT RESOURCE – An outside resource that is automatically charged upon receipt of a purchase order.

PURCHASE ORDER (PO) REVISION – A number that distinguishes printed purchase order versions. Purchasing automatically sets the revision to 0 when you initially create a purchase order. Each purchase order you print displays the current revision number.

PURCHASE ORDER (PO) SHIPMENT – A schedule for each purchase order line composed of the quantity you want to ship to each location. You can also provide delivery dates for each shipment line. You can create an unlimited number of shipments for each purchase order line. You receive goods and services against each shipment line.

PURCHASE PART – A part purchased from a supplier.

PURCHASE PART VARIANCE (PPV) – The difference in price between what was paid to the supplier and the standard cost of that item.

Glossary of Purchasing Terms

PURCHASE PLAN – Many firms develop an annual purchase plan for each major class of materials purchased. Such a plan involves an analysis of expected demand, analysis of the supply market, analysis of specific suppliers, sometimes value analysis of the item, and development of a budget. These activities then culminate in the development of purchasing plan objectives and specific purchasing strategies. Subsequent purchasing actions during the year are based on this plan.

PURCHASE REQUISITION – A document conveying authority to the procurement department to purchase specified materials in specified quantities within a specified time.

PURCHASED ITEM – An item that you buy and receive. If an item is also an inventory item, you may also be able to stock it. (See: inventory item)

PURCHASING – One of the major business functions of any organization. The function typically is responsible for acquisition of required materials, services, and equipment used in the organization.

PURCHASING AGENT – The person authorized by the company to purchase goods and services for the company.

PURCHASING CAPACITY – The act of buying capacity or machine time from a supplier.

PURCHASING DOCUMENTS – Any document you use in the purchasing life cycle, including requisitions, RFQs, quotations, purchase orders, and purchase agreements.

PURCHASING LEAD TIME – The total lead time required to obtain a purchased item. Included are procurement lead time, supplier lead time, transportation time, receiving, inspection and put away time.

PURCHASING PERFORMANCE MEASURES

- **Administrative Performance:**

$$\text{Cost Per Order} = \frac{\text{Administrative Costs + Processing + All Hands + Overhead}}{\text{Number of Orders Placed}}$$

$$\text{Purchase Cost Ratio} = \frac{\text{Actual Administrative Costs + Contribution+ Overhead}}{\text{Monetary Value of Purchases}}$$

- **Buyer's Service Level:**

$$= \frac{\text{Out of Stocks}}{\text{Potential Total Sales}} \times 100$$

- **Competition:**

$$\text{Lack of Competition} = \frac{\text{Monetary Value of Orders Placed with Sole Suppliers}}{\text{Monetary Value of Total Purchases}} \times 100$$

Glossary of Purchasing Terms

PURCHASING PERFORMANCE MEASURES

- **Cost Reduction:**

$$= \frac{\text{Current Purchase Price}}{\text{Prior Standard Price}}$$

- **Cost Savings:**

$$\text{Cost Avoidance Ratio} = \frac{\text{Actual Purch. Price} \cdot \text{Quantity Purch.}}{\text{Lowest Price Quoted} \cdot \text{Quantity Purch.}}$$

$$\text{Cost Savings Ratio} = \frac{\text{Cost Savings}}{\text{Cost of Purchasing Dept.}}$$

$$\text{N Value} = \frac{\text{Number of Shipments Rejected} + \text{Demerit Value}}{\text{Total Number of Shipments}}$$

- **Current Month Expense Variance:**

$$= \frac{\text{Actual Monthly Expense} - \text{Monthly Budget}}{\text{Monthly Budget}} \times 100$$

PURCHASING PERFORMANCE MEASURES

- **Dollars On Hand By Location/Number of SKUs:**

$$\text{Dollar Inventory Investment by Plant} = \frac{\text{Inventory On Hand By Location}}{\text{Number of SKUs}}$$

- **Early Shipment Inventory Analysis:**

$$\text{Early Shipment Analysis} = \frac{\text{Total \# of Early Shipm'ts} + \text{Value of Shipm'ts}}{\text{Total Number of Deliveries}}$$

- **Establishing Purchasing Workload:**

Standard = Number of Hours/Document

(Established through historical data and time study – includes request for negotiations, purchase order placement, write up and order entry.)

$$\text{Number of Documents/ Week} = \frac{\text{\# of Hrs. Per Week Per Buying Activity}}{\text{Standard}}$$

$$\text{Number of Docs. Per Year Per Buyer} = \text{\# of Docs. Per Week} \cdot \text{49 Wks. Per Year}$$

PURCHASING PERFORMANCE MEASURES

• **Establishing Purchasing Workload Cont.:**

$$\text{Planned Number of Buyers} = \frac{\text{Projected Workload Per Year}}{\text{\# of Docs. Per Year Per Buyer}}$$

• **Inventory Activity By Plant:**

$$\text{Inventory Activity} = \frac{\text{Average Inventory Movement By Plant(s)}}{\text{Total of All Inventory On Hand}}$$

• **Measuring Customs, Duty, and Freight:**

$$= \frac{\text{Percentage of Duties Collected Associated with International Business}}{\text{Total Business Activity}}$$

• **Number of Line Items Issued:**

$$= \frac{\text{Number of Individual SKUs Processed}}{\text{Total Number of SKUs Available}} \times 100$$

PURCHASING PERFORMANCE MEASURES

- **Price Proficiency:**

$$\text{Ratio of Price Difference} = \frac{\text{Actual Price}}{\text{Planned Price}}$$

$$\text{Total Price Difference} = [(\text{Actual Price} - \text{Planned Price}) \bullet \text{Quantity Purchased}]$$

- **Procurement Acquisition Cost:**

$$\text{Acquisition Cost} = R + P + I + S + T + L + IS + SF + E$$

Where:

R = Receiving Cost   L = Lead Time
P = PO Processing Cost   IS = Information System
I = Inspection Test Cost   SF = Space (Square Footage)
S = Staffing Cost   E = Education and Training
T = Transit Cost

Note: A company must calculate a value for each function or element.

- **Product Flow:**

$$\text{Critical Factor} = \frac{\text{Number of Urgent Orders}}{\text{Total Number of Orders Placed}}$$

$$\text{Reliability Factor} = \frac{\text{Number of Orders Delivered on Date Planned}}{\text{Total Number of Orders Placed}}$$

95

Glossary of Purchasing Terms

PURCHASING PERFORMANCE MEASURES

- **Regulatory, Societal, and Environmental Criteria:**

$$\text{Percentage of Local Business Activity} = \frac{\text{Total Number of Local Business}}{\text{Total Supplier Base}} \times 100$$

$$\text{Minority Business Activity} = \frac{\text{Minority Owned Business}}{\text{Total Business Ownership}} \times 100$$

$$\text{Women Owned Business} = \frac{\text{Total \# of Women Owned Businesses}}{\text{Total Supplier Base}} \times 100$$

- **Supplier Expediting Summary:**

$$= \frac{\text{Number of Orders Expedited (30 Days)}}{\text{Number of Orders Received (30 Days)}} \times 100$$

PURCHASING PERFORMANCE MEASURES

• **Supplier Performance:**

$$\text{Availability} = \frac{\text{Number of Times When Goods Were Available From the Supplier When Ordering}}{\text{Number of Orders Placed With the Supplier}}$$

$$\frac{\text{Ratio of}}{\text{Rejection}} = \frac{\text{Monetary Value of Shipments Rejected}}{\text{Monetary Value of Shipments Received}}$$

• **Supplier Quality Cost Index (SQCI):**

$$\text{SQCI} = \frac{\text{Total Purchase Value From Each Supplier} + \text{Expense Incurred Due to Each Supplier Quality Problem}}{\text{Total Purchase Value From Each Supplier}}$$

• **Workload:**

$$\text{Input Ratio} = \frac{\text{Number of Requisitions Received}}{\text{Number of Orders Placed}}$$

• **Year to Date Expense Variance:**

$$= \frac{\text{Actual YTD Expense} - \text{YTD Budget}}{\text{YTD Budget}} \times 100$$

Q

QUALITY ASSURANCE – A management function that includes establishing specifications that can be met by suppliers, utilizing suppliers that have the capability to provide adequate quality within those specifications, utilizing control processes that assure high-quality products and services, and developing the means for measuring the product, service, and cost performance of suppliers and comparing them with requirements.

QUALITY CONTROL – The segment of the quality assurance activity that measures quality performance and compares it with specification requirements as a basis for controlling output quality levels.

QUALITY INSPECTION – The act of inspecting products and services to determine whether they meet specifications.

QUANTITY ACCEPTED – The number of items you accept after inspection.

QUANTITY BASED ORDER – An order you place, receive, and pay based on the quantity, unit of measure, and price of the goods or services that you purchase.

QUANTITY DISCOUNT – An allowance determined by the quantity or dollar value of a purchase.

QUANTITY PER – The quantity of a component to be used in the production of its parent. Quantity per is used when calculating the gross requirements for production.

QUANTITY RECEIVED TOLERANCE – The percentage by which you allow quantity received to exceed quantity ordered.

QUANTITY REJECTED – The number of items you reject after inspection.

QUEUE TIME – The amount of time a job waits at a work center before set-up or work is performed on the job. Queue time is one element of total manufacturing lead time.

QUICK RESPONSE – A concept stressing the competitive advantage that encourages the integration of the supply chain, effectively linking buyers, suppliers, carriers, and retailers in tight communication and decision-making processes to ensure effective customer service.

QUOTATION – A statement of price, terms of sale, and description of goods or services offered by a supplier to a prospective purchaser; a bid. When given in response to an inquiry, it is usually considered an offer to sell.

QUOTATION REQUEST – See Request for Quotation.

QUOTATION TO EXPIRE DATE – The date at which time quotation price is no longer valid.

R

R – Range of a group of measurements.

= (Largest x_i in sample) - (Smallest x_i in sample)

$\overline{\text{R}}$ – Average of a sample of ranges. Center line of Range Chart.

$$= \frac{\text{Sum of all R's}}{\text{Number of Samples}}$$

REBATE – A legitimate refund to a purchasing organization in consideration for the purchase of a stipulated quantity or dollar volume within a specified time frame.

RECEIPT – A shipment from one supplier that can include many items ordered on many purchase orders.

RECEIPT EXCEPTION – A control that you can set to indicate to your accounts payable group that you want to place the corresponding invoice on hold until further notice. You designate whether your purchase order shipment should be a receipt exception when you receive the item.

RECEIPT LINE – An individual receipt transaction that identifies receipt of an item against a purchase order shipment.

RECEIPT ROUTING – A method of simplifying transaction entry by specifying routing steps for receipts.

RECEIPT TRAVELER – An internal routing ticket you place on received goods to show their final destination.

RECEIVING – This function includes the physical receipt of material, the inspection of the shipment for conformance with the purchase order (quantity and damage), identification and delivery to destination, and preparing receiving reports.

RECEIVING INSPECTION – An inspection at the receiving station to determine that the correct quantity and type of material was shipped, and to ascertain the general condition of the material with respect to damage, etc. This inspection is separate from a technical inspection for quality that may subsequently be performed.

RECEIVING POINT – Location to which material is being shipped.

RECEIVING REPORT – A form used by the receiving function of a company to inform all departments of the receipt of goods purchased.

RECIPROCITY – If buyers give preference to suppliers because they are also customers, the buyers are engaging in a practice known as reciprocity. This purchasing action is illegal if it tends to restrict competition or trade.

REJECT – An option you use to indicate that you do not want to approve a document. Purchasing returns the document to its owner for modification and resubmission, if appropriate.

REJECT OVER QUANTITY TOLERANCE – An option you use to disallow receipts that exceed the tolerance level.

REJECTED INVENTORY – Inventory that does not meet quality requirements but has not yet been sent to rework, scrapped, or returned to a supplier.

REJECTION – The act of rejecting an item by the buyer's receiving inspection as not meeting the quality specification.

RELEASE – The authorization to produce or ship material that has already been ordered (i.e. blanket order).

RELEASED VALUE RATE – A transportation rate which is based on a reduced value of the shipment which, in turn, limits the carrier's liability to a lesser amount.

REORDER POINT – See Minimum Reorder Point.

REORDER POINT SYSTEM – A continuous-review inventory control system in which an order is placed whenever a withdrawal brings the inventory position to a predetermined reorder point level.

REPROMISE DATE – Revised delivery date obtained from the supplier which differs from the original contract's delivery date.

REQUEST FOR PROPOSAL (RFP) – A solicitation document used to obtain offers to be used either in a firm-bid purchasing process or in a negotiated purchasing process, as stipulated in the request.

REQUEST FOR QUOTATION (RFQ) – In the private sector, the RFQ usually is considered to be the same as the request for proposal (RFP). In some organizations, however, an RFQ is used to obtain approximate information for planning purposes. In such cases, this fact should be clearly stated in the request. In federal government purchasing, the RFQ is used only for the purpose of obtaining planning information.

REQUISITION – See Purchase Requisition.

REQUISITION APPROVAL – The act of approving the purchases of the items on a requisition. A requisition must receive the required approvals before a buyer can create purchase orders from this requisition. The approvals can come from any employee, but a requisition is fully approved only when an employee who has enough authority approves it. If you require encumbrance or budgetary control for requisitions, a requisition is fully approved only when an employee with sufficient approval authority approves and reserves funds for the requisition.

REQUISITION ENCUMBRANCE – A transaction representing an intent to purchase goods and services as indicated by the reservation of funds for a requisition. Purchasing subtracts requisition encumbrances from funds available when you reserve funds for a requisition. If you cancel a requisition, Purchasing creates appropriate reversing entries in your general ledger.

REQUISITION POOL – Requisition lines that are approved, not cancelled, and not yet on a purchase order.

REQUISITIONER – One who initiates a purchase requisition.

REQUISITION CYCLE TIME – The time it takes from the requestor generating the requisition to the time the order is placed.

RESCHEDULING – The process of changing order or operation due dates, usually as a result of their being out of phase process or customer requirements.

Glossary of Purchasing Terms

RESERVE – An action that you take to reserve funds for a purchasing document. If the document passes the submission tests and if you have sufficient authority, Purchasing reserves funds for the document.

RESOURCE PLANNING – A planning activity for long-term capacity decisions, based on the production plan and perhaps on even more gross data (e.g., sales per year) beyond the horizon for the production plan. This activity is to plan long-term capacity needs out to the period of time necessary to acquire gross capacity additions such as major factory expansion.

RESOURCE REQUIREMENTS PLANNING – The process of converting the production plan and/or the master production schedule into the impact on key resources, such as man-hours, machine hours, storage, standard cost dollars, shipping dollars, inventory levels, etc. Product load profiles or bills of resources could be used to accomplish this. The purpose of this is to evaluate the plan prior to attempting to implement it.

RETENTION – The practice of withholding a portion of the amount due a supplier until it is determined that the item purchased meets all specifications.

RETROACTIVE PRICING – A pricing decision made after some or all of the work specified under contract has been completed, based on a review of performance and recorded cost data.

RETURN – An option that lets a buyer return a requisition line and all other unpurchased requisition lines on the same requisition to the requisition preparer.

RETURN ON INVESTMENT (ROI) – The most common definition of ROI is the ratio of annual operating income to the total capital invested in the business.

RETURN TO SUPPLIER – Material that has been dispositioned, rejected by the buyer's inspection department and is awaiting shipment back to the supplier for repair or replacement.

RETURN TO VENDOR (RTV) – A transaction that allows you to return to the vendor items from a fully or partially received purchase order and receive credit for them.

REVERSE MARKETING – An aggressive approach to developing a relationship with a supplier, in which the buyer takes the initiative in making the proposal for the relationship and the specified business transaction – a reversal of the usual buyer/supplier marketing practice.

REVISION – A particular version of an item, bill of material, or routing.

REVISION QUANTITY CONTROL – A condition placed on an item that ensures that you always identify an item by its number and its revision. Certain items require tighter controls than other. For instance, you may want to control the quantities you have in inventory for an item by revision. For another item, you may just want to know the quantities you have on hand across all revisions. You keep track of inventory quantities by revision when an item is under revision quantity control. You keep track of inventory quantities by item when an item is not under revision quantity control.

ROBINSON-PATMAN ACT – A federal law that requires a supplier engaged in interstate commerce to sell the same item to all customers at the same price (assuming the same purchase quantity). Exceptions are permitted. A lower price is permitted: (1) for a larger purchase quantity, providing the seller can justify the lower price through lower costs; (2) to move obsolete or distress merchandise; or (3) to meet the lower price of local competition in a certain geographic region.

It is illegal for a buyer to knowingly induce or accept a discriminatory price.

ROUTING – A document showing the sequence of operations to be followed in a company environment for shipping an inventory item.

RUN TIME – The actual time a job is on a machine or process in manufacturing.

S

Σ – The Greek letter S (summation).

σ – The Greek letter s (sigma) – standard deviation.

$\sigma = \sqrt{\dfrac{\Sigma (\overline{x}_i - x)^2}{n - 1}}$ Formula for Standard Deviation.

σ_c – Standard deviation of the number of imperfections.

σ_p – Standard deviation of the proportion or fraction rejected.

σ_R – Standard deviation of the ranges, R's.

σ_x – Standard deviation of the individual measurements.

$\sigma_{\overline{x}}$ – Standard deviation of the averages, $\overline{X}$'s.

SAFETY CAPACITY – The planning or reserving for excess manpower and equipment above known requirements for unexpected demand. This reserve capacity is in lieu of safety stock.

SAFETY STOCK – A quantity of stock planned to be in inventory to protect against fluctuations in demand and/or supply.

SAMPLING – See Acceptance Sampling.

SALVAGE – Surplus material or equipment that has a market value and can be sold.

SCRAP MATERIAL – Residue from operations and off spec production items that cannot be reworked or used for the originally intended purposes.

SEMIFINISHED GOODS – Products which have been stored uncompleted awaiting final operations.

SERVICE PARTS – Parts used for the repair and/or maintenance of an assembled product.

SET-UP COST – The costs incurred with changing over a machine.

SET-UP TIME – The time measured from the last good part to the first good part produced off the next manufacturing run at full efficiency.

SHARP PRACTICE – Indirect misrepresentation, unscrupulous shrewdness, deceit or trickery, just short of actual fraud. Such actions are usually designed for short-term gain, but typically act to the detriment of good long-term supplier relations based on honesty, truth, and respect.

SHERMAN ACT – The Sherman Antitrust Act of 1890 makes it illegal for parties to act in combination, conspiracy, or collusion with the intent of restricting trade in interstate commerce.

SHIP-TO-WIP – Product shipped directly to work-in-process.

SHIPMENT RELEASE – An actual order of goods and services against a planned purchase order. The planned purchase order determines the characteristics of the items on the order. The planned purchase order also has the expected quantities, prices, ship-to locations, and delivery dates for the items on the order. You identify a shipment release by the combination of the planned purchase order number and the release number. Each planned purchase order line can have multiple shipments and you can distribute the quantity of each shipment across multiple accounts.

SHIPPING – Includes packaging, marking, weighing, routing, and loading materials for transportation from one location to another.

SHIPPING LEAD TIME – The number of working days normally required for goods in transit between a shipping and receiving point, plus acceptance time in days at the receiving point.

SHIPPING POINT – The location from which material is shipped.

SHIPPING RELEASE – A form used by the purchaser to specify shipping instructions for goods purchased for delivery at a future date.

SINGLE MINUTE EXCHANGE OF DIE (SMED) – A method of set-up reduction in which the amount of time is reduced to a single digit, that is, nine minutes or less.

SINGLE SOURCE – A single supplier that you choose to buy from, although other suppliers exist.

SIX SIGMA – A statistical term which designates the achievement of only 3.4 defective components for every 1,000,000 components produced.

SOLE SOURCE – A sole supplier is one that is unique; literally the only source.

SOLICITATION – The complete document requesting potential suppliers to make offers to the buyer. One of the critical documents in the solicitation is the specification/statement of work.

In public sector sealed bidding, the solicitation generally is called an Invitation for Proposals (IFP); in negotiated procurement, it is called either a Request for Proposal (RFP) or a Request for Quotation (RFQ).

SOURCING – The action of identifying a purchasing source or supplier for goods or services. To identify the best sources for your purchases, you can create RFQs that you send to your suppliers, enter quotations from your suppliers, and evaluate these quotations for each item you purchase.

SPECIFICATION – A description of the technical requirements for a material, product, or service that includes the criteria for determining whether these requirements are met. A specification may describe the performance parameters which a supplier has to meet, or it may provide a complete design disclosure of the work or job to be done. Specifications for service contracts normally take the form of a statement of work.

SPECULATIVE BUYING – Purchasing material in excess of current and future known requirements, with the intention of profiting on price movement.

SPLIT DELIVERY – A method by which a larger quantity is ordered but delivery is spread out over several dates.

SPLIT LOT – A manufacturing order quantity that has been divided into smaller quantities.

SPONSOR – The individual that charters the process improvement team to investigate an opportunity.

SPREAD AND TARGET WORKSHEET – A statistical tool which provides a precise and quick overall picture of how a process is performing and analytical paths to pursue when problems do exist.

STANDARD COSTS – The normal expected cost of an operation, process, or product including labor, material, and overhead charges, computed on the basis of past performance costs, estimates, or work measurement.

STANDARD HOURS – The time in hours required to perform a task. It is the most common unit of measure for capacity.

STANDARD NOTE – A long note that you define for Manufacturing and later reference on as many documents as you want.

STANDARD PURCHASE ORDER – A type of purchase order you issue when you order delivery of goods or services for specific dates and locations for your company. Each standard purchase order line can have multiple shipments and you can distribute the quantity of each shipment across multiple accounts. (See: purchase order)

STANDARD RECEIPT – A receipt routing in which shipments are received into a receiving location and then delivered in a separate transaction. Standard receipts can be inspected or transferred before delivery.

STANDARD UNIT CONVERSION – The conversion formula you define between different units from the same unit class. You define your own standard conversion.

STANDARD UNIT COST – The unit cost that you may use to cost all material and resource transactions in your inventory and work-in-process system. This cost represents the expected cost for a component or assembly for a specified interval of time. The basis for standard cost may be the cost history, purchase order history, or predicted changes in future costs.

STANDARDIZATION – The process of developing standards by means of which a large variety of similar items are reduced to a minimal variety that meets all usage requirements. Inventory costs and investment costs usually are reduced in the process.

STANDING ORDER – See Open-End Order.

STATEMENT OF WORK – A statement outlining the specific services a contractor is expected to perform, generally indicating the type, level, and quality of service, as well as the time schedule required.

STATISTICAL PROCESS CONTROL (SPC) – The collection of statistical data which is used to determine whether a process is in control, that is, performing within acceptable limits.

STOCK – Stored products or service parts ready for use.

STOCK CATALOGUE BY EQUIPMENT ID – For each equipment, show stock number details of parts carried in inventory.

STOCK KEEPING UNIT – An identification with a specific part number for each end product.

STOCK LEVEL – The desired quantity of stock to be carried.

STOCK OUT – Occurs when items normally carried in stock are exhausted.

STOCK REORDER LIST REPORT – Shows all the stock items that have hit their Minimum Reorder Point or dropped below it, on that day.

STOCK STATUS – A report showing the inventory quantity on hand.

STOCKLESS PURCHASING – A general practice whereby the buyer negotiates a purchasing arrangement, including price, for a group of items for a predetermined time period, and the supplier holds the inventory until the buyer places orders for specific items. Blanket orders, open-end orders, and systems contracts can be used as stockless purchasing techniques.

STOP-OVER PRIVILEGE – A transportation arrangement whereby the shipper (supplier or buyer) can stop at stations en route to complete loading or partial unloading, or take advantage of other transit privileges.

STORE-DOOR DELIVERY – Delivery to the consignee's receiving platform by motor vehicle or rail car.

STRATEGIC ALLIANCE – See Supplier Partnership.

STRATEGIC BUSINESS UNIT (SBU) – Many large firms divide their businesses into some type of strategic business units and break strategic planning into two types of strategy: business unit strategy and corporate strategy. While corporate strategy addresses the composition of a firm's portfolio of business units, SBU strategy focuses on activities in individual SBU or industry group.

SUBASSEMBLY – A component or assembly which is used at a higher level to make up another assembly.

SUBCONTRACT – A tactic to reduce the factory work load by contracting it to another manufacturer.

SUBSTITUTE RECEIPT – An option that lets you receive predefined acceptable substitutes for any item.

SUMMARY MESSAGE ACTION – A message representing one or more exceptions. The message may include introductory and closing paragraphs separated by the exceptions listed in a columnar report format.

SUPPLIER – A company or individual that supplies goods or services.

SUPPLIER ALTERNATE – Other than the primary supplier. The alternate supplier may or may not supply a percentage of the items purchased, but is usually approved to supply the items.

SUPPLIER CERTIFICATION – A long-term commitment by a supplier to produce and deliver goods and services which conform to the customer's requirements 100% of the time. Supplier agrees to work with the customer to continuously improve its performance levels.

SUPPLIER DEVELOPMENT – A systematic organizational effort to create and maintain a network of competent suppliers and to improve various supplier capabilities that are necessary for the purchasing organization to meet its increasing competitive challenges.

SUPPLIER EVALUATION – Objective analysis of either existing suppliers by evaluating past performance, or as a preliminary assessment of potential new suppliers. Suppliers typically are evaluated on the basis of their technical quality, delivery, service, cost, and managerial capabilities.

SUPPLIER LEAD TIME – The time that normally elapses between the time an order is placed with the supplier and shipment of the material.

SUPPLIER MEASUREMENT – The act of measuring the supplier's performance to the contract. Measurements usually cover delivery, quality, and total cost.

SUPPLIER NUMBER – A numerical code used to identify one supplier from another supplier.

SUPPLIER PARTNERSHIP – A supplier partnership between a purchasing and a supplying firm involves a mutual commitment over an extended time horizon to work together to the mutual benefit of both parties in the relationship. These relationships require a clear understanding of expectations, open communication and information exchange, mutual trust, and a common direction for the future. Such relationships are a collaborative business activity that does not involve the formation of a legal partnership. The term strategic alliance is used by many firms to mean the same thing as a supplier partnership. In some firms, however, the term strategic alliance is used to describe a more inclusive relationship involving the planned and mutually advantageous joint utilization of additional operating resources of both firms.

SUPPLIER PERFORMANCE REPORT – A record of supplier quality, delivery, and service performance.

SUPPLIER PRODUCT NUMBER – The number your supplier assigns to an item. You and your supplier can have different item naming conventions. You can identify the item with one number (Item) while your supplier identifies this item using another number (Supplier Product Number). Using and referencing supplier product numbers helps you speed up your purchasing cycle. By referencing a number your supplier knows, you can help your supplier understand your purchase orders and RFQs better.

SUPPLIER PURCHASING HOLD – A hold condition you place on a supplier to prevent new purchasing activity on the supplier. You cannot approve purchase orders for suppliers you placed on hold.

SUPPLIER QUOTATION LIST – A list of suppliers who can provide goods or services you need. You often define a supplier quotation list for an item or class of items. You can use a supplier quotation list to generate multiple copies of a RFQ automatically and to manage supplier responses.

SUPPLIER RATING SYSTEM – A system used to evaluate and rate suppliers' performances, which generally involves quality, service, delivery, and price. Rating formulas vary depending upon the nature of the item being purchased, the quality required, and competition within the supplying industry.

SUPPLIER SELECTION – A process by which suppliers are evaluated according to a set of criteria to determine whether they are capable of entering a Supplier Certification process.

SUPPLIER STRATEGY – The tactics and strategy used by a company to identify and work with suppliers who will be able to attain World Class standards.

SUPPLIER SUPPLIED COMPONENT – A component item on a bill of material supplied to work-in-process directly by a supplier.

SUPPLIER SURVEY – A rigorous appraisal of a supplier's operations which includes site visits. The intent is to determine whether the supplier has its operations under control and if the supplier can enter into a partnership.

SUPPLIERS AS PARTNERS (SAP) – A program in which a company enrolls its suppliers in a program where each party enters a mutually beneficial partnership.

SUPPLY MANAGEMENT (SM) – A systems management concept employed by some organizations, designed to optimize the factors of material costs, quality, and service. This is accomplished by consolidating the following operating activities: purchasing, transportation, warehousing, quality assurance for incoming materials, inventory management, and internal distribution of materials. These activities normally are combined in a single department, similar to the arrangement under a material management form of organization.

SURPLUS AND SCRAP DISPOSAL – The function of disposing of or reclaiming scrap and surplus goods. Common methods used are: reclamation for use in operations, use elsewhere in the firm, selling to another firm, returning to suppliers, utilizing scrap dealers and brokers, sale of surplus items to employees, donation to

117

institutions, and discarding or destroying the goods. (See: investment recovery)

SWITCH TRADING – This term refers to the use of a third-party trading house in a countertrade arrangement, in which switch traders frequently trade countertrade credits for cash and the trading house sells the credits to another country that needs the goods in that particular country.

SYSTEMS CONTRACT – A contract generated by the purchasing department that authorizes designated employees of the buying firm, using a predetermined release system, to place orders directly with the supplier for specified materials during a given contract period. In the public sector, this type of contract is often called an indefinite-delivery type or "term" contract. A systems contract typically is an extension and a more sophisticated form of a blanket order.

T

TARIFF – A listing of carrier rates, accessorial charges, and rules.

TEAM – A group of knowledgeable, usually multi-functional, individuals that has been selected to work together, by pooling their resources, on a particular improvement opportunity.

TEAM LEADER – The team member who manages the team's process, and links the team to the sponsor, as well as being the primary contact for those "outside" the boundaries of the formal team.

TERMS AND CONDITIONS – A general term used to describe all of the provisions and agreements of a contract.

THEORETICAL INVENTORY – In a simple inventory system, this is the sum of one-half the lot sizes plus the reserve stock in formula calculations.

THIRD-PARTY NETWORK – In EDI operations, a third-party network firm functions as a central communications clearinghouse, much as a central check clearinghouse functions in the banking industry. It accepts the buyer's purchase orders, separates them by supplier, and at appropriate times transmits them to the computer in each supplier's organization. In addition the firm can provide format translation and other value-added functions.

THIRD-PARTY SERVICES – Services performed by any person or firm other than the buyer and supplier.

Examples include transportation, public warehousing, brokerage services, rate auditing firms, and third-party network services in EDI data transmission.

THREE-WAY MATCHING – Purchasing performs three-way matching to verify the purchase order, receipt, and invoice information match within tolerance.

TIME-AND-MATERIALS CONTRACTS – Such contracts typically provide for the acquisition of services on the basis of: (1) direct labor hours at specified fixed hourly rates that include wages, overhead, general and administrative expenses, and profit and (2) materials, generally at cost, including, if appropriate, material handling costs.

TOOLS – Those process aids that are available to assist in solving problems and making decisions by process improvement teams.

TOTAL COST – Sometimes called "all-in costs." In purchasing, total cost generally includes the price of the purchase and transportation cost, plus indirect handling, inspection, quality, rework, maintenance, incremental operations, and all other "follow-on" costs associated with the purchase.

TOTAL-PRODUCTION CYCLE TIME – Total activity time required to produce one unit of product.

TOTAL QUALITY CONTROL (TQC) – A process whereby a company commits itself to doing it right the first time, that is, it builds products or provides services in conformance to requirements.

TOTAL QUALITY MANAGEMENT (TQM) – An integration of management techniques, improvement efforts, and technical tools which focuses on continuous process improvement activities involving everyone in both the buying and supplying firms. An integrated effort toward improving quality performance at every level.

TOTAL QUANTITY ACCEPTED – The total number of accepted items for the receipt line.

TOTAL REQUISITION LIMIT – The maximum amount you authorize an employee to approve for a specific requisition.

TRADE ACCEPTANCE – A time draft or bill of exchange for the amount of purchase, drawn by the seller on the buyer, bearing the buyer's acceptance and the place of payment.

TRADE DISCOUNT – One or more reductions from list price allowed various classes of buyers and distributors.

Key criteria for classifying buying organizations are: (1) the purpose for which the material is purchased (fabrication, end use, export, resale, etc.) and (2) the form of the supplier's distribution organization and the specific marketing or distribution functions performed by the buying organization.

TRADE TERMS – Conditions offered, or offered and accepted, as terms for a sale or for payment for goods or services.

TRAILER-ON-FLATCAR – A rail-truck service whereby a highway trailer is loaded onto a rail flatcar and transported to the major destination city. At this point a tractor picks up the trailer and delivers it to the final destination.

TRANSIT TIME – An allowance given on any order for the physical movement of items from one place to the next.

TRANSHIPPING – Transferring goods from one transportation line to another.

TRAVELING (PURCHASE) REQUISITION – A purchase requisition designed for repetitive use (e.g. inventory items). It contains stock level data, potential supplier, lead times, and frequently prices and predetermined order quantities, as well as other data needed for ordering. The reusable requisition is sent to the purchasing department where a purchase order is prepared directly from it. Originally used in manual systems, the concept can also be used in computerized systems.

TWO-BIN SYSTEM – A simple, manual inventory system in which an item's inventory is stored in two different locations, with the first bin being the place where inventory is first drawn. When the first bin becomes empty (the signal to place a new order), the second bin provides backup to cover the demand until a replenishment order arrives.

TWO-WAY MATCHING – Purchasing performs two-way matching to verify that purchase order and invoice information match within tolerance.

U

UCL – Upper Control Limit.

UCL$_R$ – Upper Control Limit for Ranges.

$$= D_4\bar{R}$$

UCL$_{\bar{x}}$ – Upper Control Limit for Averages.

$$= X + A_2\bar{R}$$

USL – The upper engineering specification limit.

UN NUMBER – An identifier for a hazardous material. Each identification number has a description. Identification numbers are not unique. For instance, the same UN Number may correspond to two closely related but different types of materials.

UNIFORM COMMERCIAL CODE (UCC) ARTICLE 2 – A codification of law which clarifies and regulates the rights and obligations of buyers and sellers engaging in commercial transactions. It has been adopted by all states except Louisiana.

UNIFORM FREIGHT CLASSIFICATION – A listing of commodities showing the assigned class rates to be used in determining rail freight rates, together with government rules and regulations.

UNILATERAL CONTRACT – A contract that is formed when an offer (normally that of the buyer) is accepted through performance (normally by the supplier). This is a common process for purchasing transactions, unless an acknowledgment or other acceptance form is requested.

UNIT OF ISSUE – A unit of measurement in which an item is issued from stock.

UNIT OF MEASURE (UOM) [PURCHASING] – The unit used to purchase an item. This may or may not be the same unit of measure used in the internal systems.

UNIT OF MEASURE CLASS – A group of units of measure and their corresponding base unit of measure. The standard unit classes are: Length, Weight, Volume, Area, Time and Pack.

UNIT OF MEASURE CONVERSIONS – Numerical factors that enable you to perform transactions in units other than the primary unit of the item being transacted.

UNIT PRICE – A price associated with each individual unit of an inventory item.

UNORDERED RECEIPT – A site option that lets you receive an unordered item. You can later match an unordered item to an existing purchase order or add the unordered item to a new purchase order.

USE AS IS – Material that has been dispositioned as unacceptable per the specifications; however, the material can be used within acceptable tolerance levels.

USAGE – An attribute of your standard and one-time notes that determines how Purchasing should handle them.

UTILIZATION – The percent of elapsed time a work center is active.

V

VALUE ADDED – The value added to a product or service at each stage of its production and distribution based on its increased value at that stage.

VALUE ANALYSIS – The systematic use of techniques that serve to identify required function, to establish a value for that function, and finally to provide that function at the lowest total cost.

VALUE BASIS – An attribute you associate with a line type to indicate whether you order items for this line type by quantity or amount.

VALUE ENGINEERING – A value analysis conducted at the design stage of the product development process.

VALUE MANAGED RELATIONSHIP (VMR) – A term used for a long-term agreement with a specific supplier. Emphasis is on quality and on-time delivery and a supplier partner who lends value to the business process.

VARIABLE COSTS – Operating costs that vary directly with production volume.

VARIANCE – 1. The difference between the expected and the actual.

2. In statistics, the variance is a measure of dispersion of data.

VENDOR – A source of procurement limited to one-time buys, i.e., hot dog vendors, peanut and popcorn vendors, and t-shirt vendors.

VISUAL INSPECTION – A term generally used to indicate inspection performed without the aid of test instruments.

VOUCHER – A written instrument that bears witness to an act. Generally a voucher is an instrument showing services have been performed, or goods purchased, and authorizes payment to be made to the supplier.

W

WAIT TIME – The time that material would sit after being produced at an operation while it waits to be moved.

WARRANTY – An undertaking, either expressed or implied, that a certain fact regarding the subject matter of a contract is presently true or will be true. The word should be distinguished from "guarantee" which means a contract or promise by one person to answer for the performance of another.

WASTE – Anything other than the absolute minimum resources of material, machines and manpower required to add value to the product.

WAYBILL – A document prepared at a shipment's point of origin showing point of origin, destination, route, consignor, consignee, description of the shipment, and the amount charged for transportation.

WEIGHT, GROSS – Total combined weight of the article, container, and packing material.

WEIGHT, NET – Weight of the container or the cargo of a vehicle.

WEIGHT, TARE – Combined weight of an empty container and packing materials.

WHAT IF ANALYSIS – The process of evaluating alternative strategies. Answering the consequences of changes to forecasts, manufacturing plans, inventory levels, etc. Some companies have the capability of submitting various plans as a "trial fit" in order to find the best one. (Syn. simulation)

WORK CENTER – A specific production facility, consisting of one or more people and/or machines, which can be considered as one unit for purposes of capacity requirements planning and detailed scheduling.

WORLD CLASS – Being the best at what you do. Product, Process, or Service.

WORK-IN-PROCESS (WIP) – Product in various stages of completion throughout the plant including raw material that has been released for initial processing and completely processed material awaiting final inspection and acceptance as finished product or shipment to a customer.

X

x_i – Individual measurement.

X – Individual measurement.

$\overline{X}$ – Average of individuals within sample.

$$= \frac{\text{Sum of all the } x_i\text{'s in sample}}{\text{Sample size}}$$

$\overline{\overline{X}}$ – Average of sample averages, grand average. Center line of control chart.

$$= \frac{\text{Sum of all the } \overline{X}\text{'s}}{\text{Number of } \overline{X}\text{'s}}$$

Y

YIELD – The ratio of usable material from a process compared to the manufacturing capacity plan.

Z

Z – Standardized variate – in terms of standard deviations.

ZERO-BASE BUDGETING – An operating, planning, and budgeting process in which each manager must begin each budgeting period with no predetermined allocations, and must justify all proposed expenditures.

ZERO-BASE PRICING – A form of cost analysis based on reviewing all cost elements and working with suppliers to reduce the total combined cost of purchased material, equipment, labor, and services.

ZERO DEFECTS – Free of defects; 100% quality. A program in which quality levels and performance meet requirements 100% of the time.

ZERO INVENTORY – Condition in which there is no excess inventory in warehouses or on the floor and production is fed by J.I.T. delivery of products or material with no defects.

$\sqrt{}$ – Square root.

PURCHASING ACRONYMS:

- **ABC** – Activity Based Costing
- **B.O.A.** – Basic Ordering Agreement
- **C&F** – Cost and Freight
- **C.I.F.** – Cost, Insurance, and Freight
- **C/L** – Carload
- **C.O.D.** – Cash on Delivery
- **CRP** – Capacity Requirements Planning
- **CTM** – Cycle Time Management
- **CWT** – Hundredweight
- **DFP** – Design for Producibility
- **EDI** – Electronic Data Interchange
- **EFT** – Electronic Funds Transfer
- **EOQ** – Economic Order Quantity
- **ERP** – Enterprise Resource Planning
- **ESI** – Early Supplier Involvement
- **FAR** – Federal Acquisition Regulation
- **F.A.S.** – Free Along Side
- **FIFO** – First-In-First-Out
- **FISH** – First-In-Still-Here
- **F.O.B.** – Free on Board
- **ICC** – Interstate Commerce Commission
- **IFPMM** – International Federation of Purchasing Materials Management
- **J.I.T.** – Just-In-Time

Glossary of Purchasing Terms

- **KD** – Knocked Down
- **L.C.L.** – Less-than-Carload
- **L.T.L.** – Less-than-Truckload
- **LIFO** – Last-In-First-Out
- **MBE** – Minority Business Enterprise
- **MPS** – Master Production Schedule
- **MRO** – Maintenance, Repairs and Operating Supplies
- **MRP I** – Material Requirements Planning
- **MRP II** – Manufacturing Resource Planning
- **N.O.S.** – Not Otherwise Specified
- **O.E.M.** – Original Equipment Manufacturer
- **OSWO** – Oh Shoot! We're Out!
- **O.S. & D.** – Over, Short, & Damage Report
- **OTC** – One Touch Changeover
- **PM** – Preventive Maintenance
- **PO** – Purchase Order
- **POR** – Planned Order Release
- **PPM** – Parts Per Million
- **PPV** – Purchase Part Variance
- **P.U. & D.** – Pick Up and Delivery
- **RFP** – Request for Proposal
- **RFQ** – Request for Quotation
- **ROI** – Return on Investment
- **RTV** – Return to Vendor

- **RTV** – Return to Vendor
- **SAP** – Suppliers as Partners
- **SBU** – Strategic Business Unit
- **SKU** – Stock Keeping Unit
- **SM** – Supply Management
- **SMED** – Single Minute Exchange of Die
- **SPC** – Statistical Process Control
- **TOFC** – Trailer-on-Flatcar
- **TQC** – Total Quality Control
- **TQM** – Total Quality Management
- **UCC** – Uniform Commercial Code
- **UOM** – Unit of Measure
- **VMR** – Value Managed Relationship
- **WIP** – Work-in-Process
- **WO** – Work Order

Bibliography

Glossary of Key Purchasing Terms, Tempe, AZ: National Association of Purchasing Management.

Grieco, Jr., Peter L. et al., *Just-In-Time: In Pursuit of Excellence*, West Palm Beach, FL: PT Publications, 1988.

Grieco, Jr., Peter L., *Supplier Certification II: A Handbook for Achieving Excellence Through Continuous Improvement*, West Palm Beach, FL: PT Publications, 1993.

Grieco, Jr., Peter L., *Supply Management Toolbox: How to Manage Your Suppliers*, West Palm Beach, FL: PT Publications, 1995.

Grieco, Jr., Peter L. and Hine, Paul G., *The World of Negotiations: Never Being a Loser*, West Palm Beach, FL: PT Publications, 1991.

Oracle Purchasing™ Reference Manual Release 10, Volume 4, Redwood Shores, CA: Oracle Corporation, 1994.

Pilachowski, Mel J., *Performance Measurements: A Roadmap for Excellence*, West Palm Beach, FL: PT Publications, 1995.

Statistical Process Control Seminar, Professionals For Technology Associates, Inc.